STORES
OF THE YEAR

no.19

STORES

OF THE YEAR

no.19

RSD Publishing, Inc., 302 Fifth Avenue, New York, NY

RSD Publishing, Inc.
302 Fifth Avenue
New York, NY 10001
212-279-7000
CS@rsdpublishing.com
www.rsdpublishing.com

Distributors to the trade in the United States and Canada
Innovative Logistics
575 Prospect Street
Lakewood NJ 08701
732-363-5679

Distributors outside the United States and Canada
HarperCollins International
10 East 53rd Street
New York, NY 10022-5299

Library of Congress Cataloging in Publication Data:
Stores of the Year No. 19

Printed and Bound in Hong Kong
ISBN: 978-0-9854674-1-8

TABLE OF CONTENTS

Retail Design Institute International Store Design Competition

EuroShop Retail Design Awards

Retail Design International Best in Category

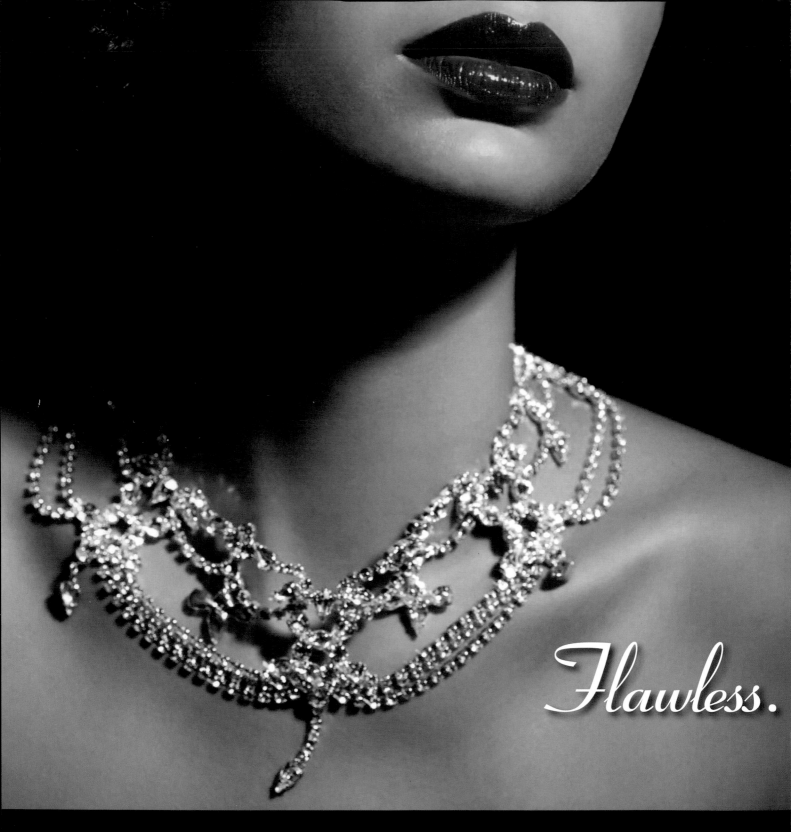

Flawless.

THE NEW OPTIMA LED® STRETCHLITE BACKLIT LIGHT BOX.
COMPLETE UNIFORMITY, CORNER TO CORNER, EDGE TO EDGE.

It offers the brilliance and uniformity of LED technology and accommodates the broadest size range of images – including large format displays that seamlessly cover an entire wall – to help you achieve unmatched visual impact. The Optima LED StretchLite also costs less to operate, requires less maintenance and is better for the environment than fluorescent. The bigger your vision, the more you need the Optima LED StretchLite.

FOREWORD

It is with great honour that I present within this book the winners of the 42nd Annual International Store Design Competition. The Retail Design Institute is the global professional community and voice that represent those of us who's careers and passions are all about delivering exceptional customer experiences and brand expressions for our clients. These experiences are illustrated by the projects chronicled in this book. The work shown is the culmination of countless hours between design studios and their clients that merge into some of the most compelling new retail designs each year. These environments will be visited by tens of millions across six continents—that's impact.

The Institute's annual retail design competition is the only peer-reviewed retail design awards and thus is recognized as the most prestigious to win. Each January the Institute hosts an awards gala in New York City during the week of the National Retail Federation's (NRF) show and conference. The evening is highlighted by an awards ceremony followed by a *féte* where the industry's most influential brands and designers come to celebrate innovative design. We would welcome you to attend and hope you will consider being part of this night in January 2014.

We encourage you to take inspiration from these projects and consider entering your own projects each year when we issue the 'call for competition' each August. Check online at www. retaildesigninstitute.org for details that are posted or feel free to write me at the address shown below.

Finally, the Institute has put together a highlight DVD of the awards and it can be utilized at your own event as part of the conversation of International Retail Design Trends. If you would like to get details of this programme please email me whereby we can discuss the details.

Enjoy the experience of design!

Brian Dyches, FRDI
International Chairman, Retail Design Institute
bdyches@retaildesigninstitute.org

PANEL OF JUDGES — 42ND ANNUAL
INTERNATIONAL STORE DESIGN COMPETITION

JUDGING CHAIR
Chen Sapirstein, The Melt & Chairman – Northern California Chapter

JUDGING CO-CHAIR
Kraig Kessel, Kraido

INTERNATIONAL CHAIRMAN
Brian Dyches, Atmospheric Experience Design

James Farnell, Little & President – Southern California Chapter
Michael Bodziner, Gensler
Heather Garcia, Nintendo
Dannielle Sergent, Sergent Studios
Diane Cuyler, FIDM S.F.
Cameron Imani, Landor

JUDGING ASSISTANTS
Vera Anderson, San Francisco State University
Jessica Hammett, Academy of Art University

GET IT TOGETHER.

The nature of retail is changing. Shopping is now a two-way, participatory engagement – and customers expect consistency and clarity whether they're online, on the move or in the store.

Successfully delivering that seamless experience?
That's Together Commerce.

Discover Toshiba's new
vision for retail engagement
at **www.toshibagcs.com**

TOGETHER
COMMERCE
™

INTRODUCTION

This, the 19th volume in our series, presents the "Stores of the Year" as a collection of award winners. First up are the Retail Design Institute's International Store Design Competition winners. The Institute presented 28 awards this year and every one is extensively featured here. Next it's the EuroShop Retail Design Awards—an award given to the retailer for coherent store concepts and clear messages regarding the product range. From a field of 26 finalists, four winners were named. And finally, we have included the *Retail Design International* Best in Category selections. The editors of the bimonthly publication, myself included, had the pleasure of selecting our picks for outstanding stores.

With all of these selections, however, emerges something more than a mere collection of winners: the stores shown here represent the retail industry's commitment to fulfill the needs of consumers in an increasingly complex shopping universe. The solutions these retailers have found are two-fold: they embrace the technology that many see as the enemy, and they give the shopper an experience that is only possible in a physical environment.

Mistral Wine Store in São Paulo, winner of the Retail Design Institute's prestigious Store of the Year award, utilizes the latest in-store digital technology to educate consumers as to the finer points of the wines on offer. In addition, the retailer has eliminated the traditional sales counter and replaced it with iPad-carrying sales associates—shoppers can "check-out" from anywhere in the store. Technology and customer service unite to create an experience that expertly presents the products while focusing completely on the consumer.

Many other stores featured here expand the definition of the retail shop and create environments that entice shoppers to linger. Liverpool Interlomas features a rooftop plaza; Aaron Brothers offers expert advise and fun-filled instruction; Ann Summers has its assortment of "goodies"; Chicago Sporto Dopot and The Manchester United Experience offer immersive team-centered experiences; PEZ Visitor Center and McCormick World of Flavors combine museum exhibits and activities; Sunglass Hut Floating Store invites shoppers onto a barge... the list keeps going and includes almost every retailer in this book. Stores are no longer just places in which to display products—although products are still most definitely displayed—they are places to relax, learn and play.

Technology that bridges the physical and digital experiences also abounds. Although technology is hardly surprising in stores such as the AT&T Flagship in Chicago, it also takes center stage in Colour with Asian Paints, New Balance Boston, Jordan Flight Lab and El Palacio de Hierro Interlomas. Retailers have learned to seamlessly connect the online and offline experience and utilize technology to connect the shopper to the brand.

With all of the changes to retailing in recent years some things, however, remain unchanged. Innovative store design and expert visual merchandising still promote merchandise as no website possibly can. Zara, Scabal, Piccino, Camper Shoes, Reischmann, engelbert strauss, De•Cor and Loblaws are all shoppers' paradises with irresistible presentation, and products, at every turn.

This collection of award winners represent the very best that retailing has to offer. Enjoy.

Judy Shepard
Associate Publisher, RSD Publishing

EMPORIO ARMANI
realized by IDW Metawood

Your Design.   Any Shape, Size, Finish.

MicroLite!™

Light Weight
Pre-Fabricated
Pre-Finished

Any Finish
Any Shape
Any Size

Save Money
Save the Earth
Save Time

THE FAN CLUB

Canopies
Clouds
Soffits
Rings
Baffles
Fascias
Beams
Trellis
Signage
Portals
etc.

COPYRIGHT KMDI 2013

PEZ Visitor Center, rgla solutions, inc.

KMDI

800 474 5004
www.KMDI.net

LIGHT CHANGES
EVERYTHING

STUDIO
SERRADURA

studioserradura.com
studioserradura.tumblr.com

Richter+Ratner *Builders Since 1912*

45W 36th Street, 12th Floor, New York, NY
212.936.4500 www.richterratner.com

R+R

Retail Design Institute™

www.retaildesigninstitute.org

- Networking
- Student Design Contest
- Career Building

- Education
- Global Access & Intelligence
- Int'l Retail Design Competition & Awards

Since 1961 – the Retail Design Institute promotes the advancement and collaborative practice of creating selling & experience environments by design professional throughout the world

PURCHASES

LIKES

BROWSED

STORE PICKUP

PRODUCT VIEWS

CLICK-THROUGHS

SEARCHED

ADD TO CART

REDEEMED OFFER

CHECK-INS

VIDEO VIEWS

THE POWER OF OMNICHANNEL PERSONALIZATION

It's 2013. Consumers demand a consistent and seamless shopping experience regardless of channel.

Certona's real-time personalization platform increases engagement and conversions by leveraging 1:1 behavioral profiling and Big Data to serve up the most individualized content, offers and product recommendations across all customer touch points.

Isn't it time you discover what true personalization can do for your business?

C E R T O N A
Personalize Anytime Anywhere℠

LEARN MORE
www.certona.com

CREATING DIGITAL DESTINATIONS

"McCormick World of Flavors is an example where digital drives design;
creating a Discovery Trail that engages, educates, and entertains the store's guests.

5th Screen Digital Services partners by defining and then exceeding expectations
on the part of JGA and the client.

More importantly, 5th Screen succeeded in doing the same with the McCormick
World of Flavors guests, by providing a dynamic series of digital destinations that
bring the story of McCormick and its family of brands to life."

Ken Nisch
Chairman – JGA

5th Screen Digital Services

"Specializing in the Impossible"

www.5thscreen.com

San Jose, C

408.440.4520

831.818.0584

Client: **TITAN** - 32% increase in revenue, 72% increase in footfall

Client: **ASIAN PAINTS** - 35% increase in regional sales

Client: **BMW** - Simultaneous rollout across 7 countries in GCC

EXPERIENTIAL DESIGN LAB

Strategy | Innovation | Technology
led by design

New Delhi | Rome | Dubai | www.experientialdesignlab.com | +91-11-41050698 | info@experientialdesignlab.com

Your Global Flagship Event.

EuroShop

The World's Leading Retail Trade Fair

16 – 20 February 2014

Düsseldorf · Germany

www.euroshop.de

Mistral Wine Store

São Paulo, Brazil

SCOPE OF THE WORK This is the first physical store for Mistral, a wine distributor that had previously sold mostly via the internet. The design directive called for the use of wine bottles as a gateway for consumers to discover the product, fulfilling the promise of a physical and justifying presence.

BRAND PROMISE Mistral is a brand that, previously to opening a store, sold wine both to top restaurants in Brazil and to experienced wine collectors. Its customers were very knowledgeable about fine wine. With the opening of its store, the brand wanted to enlarge its consumer base to include less experienced wine buyers while building a closer relationship with its established customers. The resulting store is the perfect space to fulfill both those needs, offering layers of discovery opportunities and an always changing customer experience, as the bottles are changed constantly. The brand promise is to offer a great diversity of wines, but with a very selective choice process.

STORE PLANNING The architecture is meant to recede into the background and allow the focus to be on the bottles. Though simple, the space is sensuous, with curves that evoke a wine bottle and the complexities of the world of wine. The store represents a sense of exclusivity within a universe that is open with possibilities.

WAYFINDING AND CIRCULATION The store plan is a series of interconnected spaces that offer various layers of interaction to the shopper. The further he or she penetrates the store, the more information can be had on specific wines. The pathways are quite free, new spaces appearing as the client journeys through the store.

The physical experience is quite unique, the spacing seems to be much larger through the use of curves in the layout and different ceiling heights.

OVERALL LIGHTING Probably one of the key features of the store, the light design was essential to create impressive atmospheres such as the main corridor of the entrance but also intimate spaces such as around the interactive table or in the reading space by the library. Lighting accentuates the architecture and brings attention to the bottles that immediately impacts the customer.

VISUAL MERCHANDISING The store uses the bottles themselves as a media to inform the client. The idea was conceived right from the beginning and guided the design of the store. Technology and architecture come together to sell a very traditional product in an innovative and technological way.

SALES TECHNOLOGY INTEGRATION The sales associates all carry iPads and can facilitate purchases from any area of the store, moving away from the traditional cash/wrap counter. A separate warehouse in the basement of the mall can also organize deliveries, carrying boxes to a client's car, or directly to his or her home.

GOALS AND OBJECTIVES The store uses innovative digital technology in a discrete manner, as the client may touch or move bottles to obtain information about a product. The space is conceived as a wine library, encouraging curiosity to both the experienced wine buyers and the more casual consumer. The icon of the bottle itself is the basis of the architecture, generating a new spatiality for the unique retail experience.

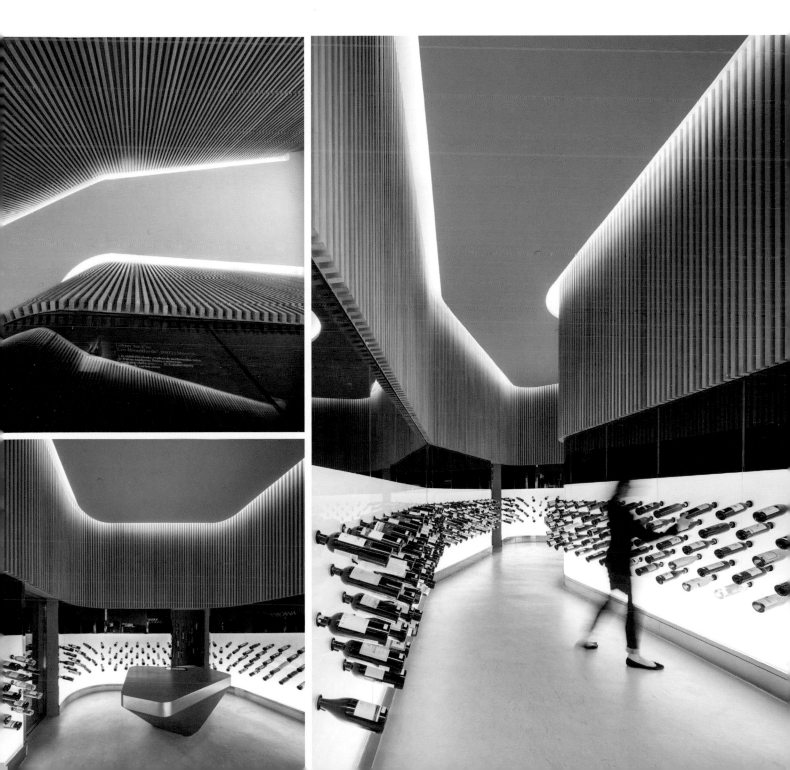

CUSTOMER JOURNEY The customer is invited by a long corridor with bottles of wine that abstractly hang in a curved glass wall. As he touches some bottles the screens show general information of each region. Other spaces of the stores allow him to get to know more about each bottle, either by talking with the sellers, using an interactive table, a vast wine library or doing wine tasting with renowned producers in a dedicated space.

FIXTURING & FINISHES One of the most unusual features of the store is the arrangement of suspended bottles seen throughout the space. From the showcase in the main corridor, to the climate controlled cave and the wall that is used as stock, the bottles are always suspended, becoming a constant presence in the store even though displayed in different manners in each space. Materials such as oak and neutral textures and colors evoke the world of wine in a discrete and elegant manner. The complex nature of the carpentry and glass work—elements had to fit within millimeters to ensure the displays work—called for exacting and highly skilled construction.

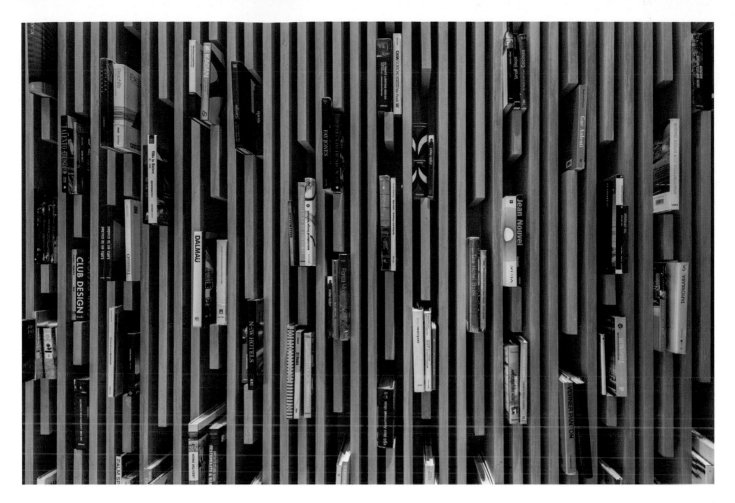

VISUAL MERCHANDISING Although the wine bottle iconology is emphasized throughout, the well-rounded sophistication of the consumer is not forgotten. One wall includes art and design books, set into the wall, as decorative elements. Shoppers can peruse the books as they explore the wine offerings.

Studio Arthur Casas São Paulo, Brazil

PROJECT AND RETAIL DESIGN TEAM
Arthur Casas
Raphael França
Joana Oliveira
Cristiane Trolesi
Gabriel Ranieri
Mariana Santoro

ARCHITECT
Studio Arthur Casas

CLIENT
Mistral

GENERAL CONTRACTOR
Souza Lima

OUTSIDE CONSULTANTS
k2P Projetos *Hydraulic Installations, Metal Structure*
Studio Serradura *Lighting*
Super Uber *Technology*

Art des Caves *Cave*
Futurebrand *Visual Branding*
Lutron *Automation*

SUPPLIERS
RB Pisos de Madeira *Wood*
Clamom *Carpentry*
Primo Vidros *Glasses*
Super Uber *Technology*
Mr Cryl *Concrete Painting*
Serradura Oikós *Lighting*
Vip Door *Automatic Door*
Herança Cultural *Furniture*
Lumini *Furniture*
Scandinavian Design *Furniture*

PHOTOGRAPHY
Fernando Guerra, FG+SG, Fotografia de Arquitectura

Liverpool Interlomas Department Store

Municipio de Huixquilucan, Estado de Mexico, Mexico

SCOPE OF WORK The design team's mission was the construction of a new flagship department store in Interlomas, a northern suburb of Mexico City. Needed were an exterior design, an interior design, and the development of a rooftop urban park and gourmet eating area. FRCH Design Worldwide was responsible for the interior design of the 29,600 m2, four-level, full-line department store. The design team strived to create an environment that would become a social center for Interlomas and afford a great shopping experience for both residents and visitors to the area. The client, Servicios Liverpool sought a new personality for the brand, resulting in a balance between the Liverpool family-friendly environment and the new fashion-oriented attitude.

GOALS ACHIEVED The new design delivers on the Liverpool brand message, "This is a store for me and my family." The store has become a fashion-forward shopping destination, as well as a place that entertains and provides a sense of community. The design is an evolution of the Liverpool brand's core values that stresses a forward-looking, fashion-oriented attitude that encourages customers to say, "Liverpool is part of my life."

CUSTOMER JOURNEY Posing a challenge to the designers was the site location and the curved shape of the building. Ultimately, however, they utilized the shape to their advantage, creating easy-to-navigate routes through the store, while making the shopper's journey dramatic and engaging. From the moment they arrive, visitors are engaged by the four-story atrium, filled with movement and filtered natural light from above. A sense of discovery is created beginning on the cool and trendy ground level and continuing up to a warm and contemporary level, the third fashion level and completing the journey at the gourmet area and roof garden.

VISUAL MERCHANDISING From the center core the design team added an entrance to each one of the worlds, creating an invitation to the customer to explore. These areas are preludes of what is to come and highlight the latest trend, while presenting the merchandise as "hero."

STORE PLANNING   The center core, or the heart of the store, uses simple but bold architecture with organic shapes to synchronize the center atrium with the surrounding departments and even the outdoors, which can be discerned through the skylight. Circulation flows around the core with wide aisles for ease of shopping. In the surrounding areas, what the designers call the "sub core," architectural focal points are created to convey the personality of the department. Long, curving lines add drama and reinforce the directional flow. The personality of each department is emphasized with lighting and the use of colors and materials.

Liverpool Interlomas' crown jewel is the rooftop park, or Sky Park, that has become a community meeting place welcoming local families and visitors alike. It sits at the top of the vertical journey that includes two levels of parking with the various shopping levels inside.

LIGHTING The lighting contributes to various looks in the different sections of the store, creating distinct atmospheres, personalities and moods. The LED-lit internal escalator in the atrium, located at the heart of the store, changes color on a continuous basis, creating a focal point for visitors. Natural light flows through the skylight.

KEY:

1 JUICE BAR (K02)

2 ICE CREAM (K01)

3 GOURMET (FF11)

4 GOURMET COFFEE (FF01)

5 BOOKS

6 SUSHI (FF05)

7 BISTRO 180 SQM

8 ITALIAN (FF03)

9 GOURMET CORNER (FF13)

10 BAKERY / PATISSERIE (FF09)

11 MOSHI CREAMS (BY OTHERS)

12 CHOCOLATIER (BY OTHERS)

13 TAPAS (FF07)

14 WINE & LIQUER

15 SEATING ZONE

16 FUN CANDY (FC01)

17 DEMO COUNTER

FINISHES The overall material palette is based on fashion and nature and becomes warmer as the shopper journeys upward from floor to floor. Contrasts between black and white on the ground level give way to neutral wood tones with dark accents, and then on to warmer wood finishes and different textures. Each of the spaces has its own personality incorporating the floors, ceiling and fixtures.

FRCH Design Worldwide Cincinnati, OH

PROJECT DESIGN TEAM
Jim Lazzari Chief Architectural Officer
Young Rok Park Vice President, Creative Director
HeeSun Kim Vice President, Creative Director
Rob Carey Senior Designer
Claudia Cerchiara Vice President, Project Manager
Joe Brumback BIM Manager
Brad Kalchek BIM Manager
Jonathan Wood BIM Manager
Annie Fugazzi BIM Coordinator
Mike Magee BIM Coordinator
Deb Casey Senior Professional, Planning and Merchandising
Lori Kolthoff Director, Resource Design
Jennifer Eng Senior Resource Design

CLIENT
Servicios Liverpool SA de CV, Mexico, D.F.

RETAIL DESIGN TEAM
Martin Perez Director
Iliana Davila General Store Planning Manager
Eumir Salgad Project Manager
Javier Roble Store Planning Manager
Luis Gonzalez Store Planning Designer
Jose Manuel Zurutuza Design Coordinator
Nuria Mucharraz Design Architect
Maria del Pilar Romero Fixture Design
C. Sofia Otto Color and Material Resources
Maria Elena Meneses Corners Manager

Maria Elena Flores Corners Coordinator
Maria de Lourdes Mendez Casares Director of Visual Presentation
Yharid Palafox Manager of Visual Presentation (Interior)
Mauricio Ruiz Visual Presentation Coordinator
Cristina Bordas Visual Presentation Coordinator

ARCHITECT INTERIOR AND EXTERIOR
Rojkind Arquitectos Mexico, D.F.

GENERAL CONTRACTOR
Servicios Liverpool SA de CV Construction Team Mexico

OUTSIDE DESIGN CONSULTANTS
Thomas Balsley Associates New York, NY
Thomas Balsley FASLA, Principal Designer, *Sky Park*
JHP Design London, UK, *Interior Gourmet, Roof Level*
Lewis Moberly London, UK, *Interior Gourmet, Roof Level*

SUPPLIERS
Studio NYL Boulder, CO, *Structural Exterior*
EMRSA Mexico, D.F. *Structural Engineer*
Agisa *Exterior Lighting*
Lighting Workshop Graphic Design *Interior Lighting Designer*
ARCO JC. Construcciones *Construction Coordinator*
Green Roof *Waterproofing*
GM Vialdi *Furniture*
PC Proyectos *Furniture*

Núcleos Integrales *Façade*
Enrique Martínez Romero *Structure*
Maheja *Brickwork*
Dedrum *Drywall*
Intecsa *Electrical*
Tepsa *Water*
Tracsa *Metal Work*
Kadensa-Retro *Furniture*
Riviera *Office*
Yvonne Iluminación *Lighting*
Chrometro *Furniture for Interior Gourmet*
Vitra *Furniture*
Maharam *Upholstry*
Terza *Upholstry*
Porcelanosa *Flooring*
Plastiglass *Acrylics/Paint*

PHOTOGRAPHY
Paúl Rivera / archphoto, Brooklyn, NY
Jaime Navarro, Mexico, D.F.
Photos of Sky Park: **Courtesy of Thomas Balsley Associates**

Shinsegae Uijeongbu

Uijeongbu, South Korea

SCOPE OF WORK Shinsegae, meaning "New World," is Korea's most prestigious department store group with a world-class reputation for innovation, service and design. The store in Busan, South Korea is even listed in the Guinness Book of Records as the biggest department store in the world. For its new store in the wealthy residential suburb of Uijeongbu, just north of Seoul city center, Shinsegae appointed JHP design consultancy to design a master-plan and develop a distinctive design language for the 12-story outlet, carrying the design through all key floors.

BRANDING Shinsegae's brand promise has always been built on tradition paired with modernity, and complete focus on the customer. Although there is a large logo on the exterior of the building, the Shinsegae branding is carried out in an understated and subtle fashion throughout the store. The logo acts as a reassurance of the high quality and reliability of the retailer.

ENVIRONMENTAL GRAPHICS The central escalator core is identified with an illuminated checkered pattern that varies in color and configuration and is used to connect the floors. As many brands have to be represented, there is plenty of scope for the tenant brands to express themselves within their own visual template.

STORE PLANNING The ground floor spans 14,000 m2 and houses cosmetics, jewelry, accessories, luxury brands, and a deli and gourmet food market. The core design philosophy includes a combination of "'identifiers" and "controlled contrasts" to ensure that the Shinsegae brand is prominent in a shopping experience that is rich with powerful brands and original products.

FIXTURING The fashion and beauty departments in the store are almost entirely "concessioned" and fixtures were supplied by the tenant brands. However, the designers set guidelines to which all had to conform. This ensured that the design proposals submitted by the various brands were in keeping with the architectural language of the interior and the aspirations of the client for excellence in customer experience. Elsewhere the merchandising fixturing is elegant, luxurious and suitably hard wearing for an extremely busy store environment.

LIGHTING The lighting strategy was to create a series of light and dark contrasts, and to use color to help guide customers around the store. The young fashion department is like a deconstructed warehouse with industrial structures and artificial roof-lights, whilst the restaurant complex on the ninth floor effectively uses the natural light from the central piazza which is used for 'al fresco' dining.

VISUAL MERCHANDISING Opportunities for visual merchandising are carefully planned, the most impactful of which exist at the base of the escalators. These large visual merchandising assemblies catch the eye and quickly summarize the offerings ahead.

BRAND PROMISE Shinsegae has a policy that each new store should surpass the standards of the previous one, regardless of location—a daunting task given the retailer's network of world-class outlets. The interior of the new space allows clear views across departments, logical customer journeys, ease of navigation, as well as surprising and enchanting moments along the way. Only

the very best international premium and luxury brands are offered in the store and they're complemented by the most luxurious finishes and materials. Of particular note are the Riven marble lift surrounds, bronzed suspended lighting and the profiled timber ceiling area above the deli, which is deliberately cut short against the clean lines of the surrounding luxury brands.

GOALS ACHIEVED Shinsegae was adamant that the new store belong to the people of Uijeongbu and not be a diluted version of the retailer's ultra-sophisticated city center stores. To meet this challenge, the design agency developed the thematic platform "Uijeongbu is my Shinsegae" as a backdrop to the overarching, modern-classic architecture. As with many Asian department stores, Uijeongbu is built over a major railway commuter intersection which guarantees a continuous flow of wealthy customers. Already a huge commercial success, the store's design and experience has been widely reported in national and general Asian media.

CUSTOMER JOURNEY The store is vertically anchored at both ends by food— a food court in the second basement and a series of upmarket restaurants on the building's top floor.

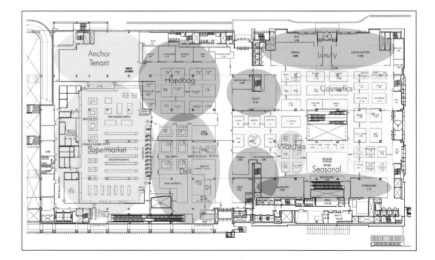

JHP London

PROJECT AND RETAIL DESIGN TEAM
For JHP:
Steve Collis Joint Managing Director
Raj Wilkinson Joint Managing Director
David Rook Director of Retail Design
Jeongho Son Senior Retail Architect
Martin Williams Senior Retail Designer

For Shinsegae:
Jooun Um Design Director
Jonghoon Kim Design Coordinator
Youngseung Ko Project Manager

GENERAL CONTRACTOR
Shinsegae internal construction company

LIGHTING
Inverse Lighting London, UK

PHOTOGRAPHY
Hee Won Cho Seoul, South Korea

Aaron Brothers
West Hollywood, CA

SCOPE OF WORK The store needed to help customers explore options, gain confidence and succeed with their art and framing projects. It was essential that the environment elevate art supplies and include a creative hotspot for artisans of all kinds. It was also important that the design provide a sense of emotion in the store, building on the reason customers create art and frame personal items.

BRAND PROMISE Aaron Brothers celebrates creativity. The concept of the "Artist's Spirit" is built on research that finds people engaged in a creative project identity themselves as artists regardless of the complexity or depth of the project. This powerful emotional connection drives the brand expression. The space celebrates customers' art and helps them frame and preserve their memories while inspiring artistic expression. It communicates a sense of exploration and conveys the technical expertise of the staff while creating a community for art creators and art lovers—bringing together people who value art and celebrating what is important to them

CUSTOMER JOURNEY Customers enter a vibrant main aisle featuring frames, art project ideas and art supplies. To the right is the Frame Workshop; to the left is Custom Framing, a private consultation area with a window into the professional frame shop through which customers can watch their art being framed by the retailer's experts. A new Art District offers everything artists might need for their studios. Included is a large Brush Bar, with brushes organized according to paint medium. The store also offers interactive, hands-on experiences: "Use Our Wall" allows customers to compose frame groupings, and Art Bar provides a place for demonstrations and guided DIY framing.

ENVIRONMENTAL GRAPHICS Artwork, including swatches of paint and canvas texture, is integrated into signage. A clear hierarchy identifies overarching departments, followed by inspirational signage and perimeter wayfinding that include graphics that are large and impactful as well as personal and approachable.

STORE PLANNING Innovative and flexible fixtures allow Aaron Brothers to inspire customers with project ideas. A gallery displays ready-to-hang wall art on an accessible ledge with stock organized below. An Inspiration Alley includes pivoting wall panels that show customers the variety of display and framing possibilities.

LIGHTING Pendant dome lights provide direct light in the framing consultation areas. The Art District, which anchors the back of the store, is lit by Edison bulbs and fluorescent flood lights above a luminous ceiling element to create the look and feel of a skylight in an artist's loft.

VISUAL MERCHANDISING An all-white collage of frames in various sizes and shapes, defines the Custom Framing area and add texture and sophistication. To emphasize the tactile element of brushes, a key category for this retailer, they are unpackaged and artfully displayed in tin cups. Playful wooden manikins reappear throughout the space.

GOALS ACHIEVED The new space is imbued with an "artist's spirit," and offers an exciting mix of merchandise, inspiration, tips and techniques. It is a hip and urban space that provides customers with an experience that inspires artistic expression. The store has three distinct zones that amplify the brand's core categories: art supplies, custom framing and do-it-yourself framing.

FIXTURING & FINISHES The store evokes an artist's loft, with polished concrete floors and fixtures of wood tones on industrial-style iron casters. Wood plank flooring highlights the center aisle and large wooden architectural beams divide the space into its three sections. Consultation areas include residential-inspired furnishings with a studio feel. The design team created an innovative selling system for ready-made frames, organizing frames by finish and size on sliding display panels so customers can first, determine the style, then the size they need. The sliding panels artfully conceal inventory, vertically stacked "shoulder-out," making restocking an effortless task for associates.

Chute Gerdeman Columbus, OH

PROJECT DESIGN TEAM
Elle Chute Co-Founder & Co-CEO
Brian Shafley President & Chief Creative Officer
Joanna Felder Vice President, Intelligence & Brand Strategy
David Birnbaum Director of Architecture
Elaine Evans Creative Director
Cindy McCoy Project Manager
Nicole Faccinto Senior Designer, Visual Strategy
Susan Siewny Vice President, Design Implementation
Steve Pottschmidt Vice President, Design Development
Katie Clements Senior Designer, Materials Specialist
Steve Williams Production Manager, Design Implementation

RETAIL DESIGN TEAM
Jim King SVP/General Manager (Michaels/Aaron Brothers)
Robin Moore VP, Store Development & Construction (Michaels)
Katy Hanson VP Marketing (Aaron Brothers)
Debra Ebel Director, Store Experience

Wendy Prebil Director, Visual Merchandising (Aaron Brothers)
Paul Scheelf Sr. Director of Store Development (Michaels)
Dan Sandoval Construction Manager (Michaels)
Connie Svoboda Manager, FF&E (Michaels)
Heather Lesley Senior Store Planner (Michaels)

CLIENT
Jim King/Aaron Brothers, Irving, TX

ARCHITECT
L&L Drafting Studio City, CA, Leslie Rodriguez

GENERAL CONTRACTOR
Just Construction & Management
Pacific Palisades, CA

OUTSIDE DESIGN CONSULTANTS
Js Yenjai Consulting Service Claremont, CA
Mack Yenjai, P.E., *Structural Engineer*

SUPPLIERS
Scofield Los Angeles, CA, *Flooring, Concrete*
Centiva Florence, AL, *Flooring, Vinyl Tile*
Interface Flor LaGrange, GA, *Flooring, Carpet Tile*
Wilsonart Temple, TX, *Laminate*
Pionite Auburn, ME, *Laminate*
Octopus Products Toronto, ON, Canada, *Laminate*
IFS Coatings Inc. Gainesville, TX, *Powdercoatings*
Glidden Professional Strongsville, OH, *Paint*
Sterling Tree Studio Archdale, NC, *Furniture, Sofa*
Hive Modern Portland, OR, *Furniture, Lounge Chairs*
Lumens Sacramento, CA, *Decorative Lighting*
The Lamp Goods *Decorative Lighting*

McCormick World of Flavors

Harborplace Light Street Pavilion, Baltimore MD

BRAND PROMISE McCormick is a global leader in the manufacture, marketing and distribution of spices, seasoning mixes, condiments and other flavorful products to "flavornistas" of all sorts from the culinary trade to the home enthusiast. Guests at the McCormick World of Flavors enjoy interactive and educational displays, cooking demonstrations and product sampling, bringing the brand to life.

GOALS ACHIEVED The design objective was to create an experiential brand showcase featuring McCormick's range of cooking, baking and grilling products. This was achieved by allowing visitors to interact with many favorite brands from around the world such as Lawry's, Old Bay, Zatarain's, Grill Mates, and Thai Kitchen, while showcasing how McCormick brings flavor to their lives every day.

CUSTOMER JOURNEY Tapping into the brand's unique legacy, the space allows real world cooking experiences with "fantasy" scenarios, such as a dream barbecue station and an area for cooking demonstrations featuring celebrity chefs, giving the sense that the kitchen is the heart of the walk-in experience. Located in Baltimore's Inner Harbor, the store itself is loft like—reminiscent of the McCormick plant and headquarters that stood steps away on the same street from 1920 to 1989. It was important for the brand to have The World of Flavors to serve not only as a corporate show case, but to further identify with the company's roots in Baltimore, the Harbor, and this location.

Signature identity elements begin at the store exterior, with the McCormick brand block that extends above the entrance with a "flavor band" and a digital screen offering a glimpse into the ongoing history, product, brands and activities within. The store is organized by a series of zones that focus on key product categories and activity areas.

LIGHTING The store benefits from natural light streaming through three glass walls surrounding the space. General lighting is kept at a low level, allowing the product-specific, focalized illumination to make the merchandise pop.

VISUAL MERCHANDISING Merchandise is displayed by specific zones related to each of the key brands, including the McCormick products and its sub-brands, each treated in unique ways. Other areas of the floor are cross-merchandised by cuisine with product groupings based on compatibility. Zones allow products to be featured or split according to the cuisine groupings. Experiential moments are showcased in vignettes, including the "red cap" alcove and the "gifting" history wall.

FINISHES The designers utilize culinary-inspired finishes, stainless steel, aluminum, marble, that provide a progressive and contemporary appearance—part test lab, part "kitchen of the future." The space has a loft-like appeal with polished concrete floors and open ceilings. The "bones" of the building serve as a background element, contrasting with the tabletops made from recycled, reclaimed wood. In the demo kitchen a unique marble top and red tile facade set off the area.

STORE PLANNING The store is organized in a series of zones that focus on branding the key product categories and activity areas. Interactive stations include five immersive digital engagements, including Guess that Spice, a game that tests the consumer's sense of smell, Flavorprint, an interactive personalized flavor profile, and Flavors in the Making, a series of entertaining videos on how spices and herbs go from plant to table. Cooking demonstrations by McCormick's house and celebrity chefs, as well as product samplings, allow visitors to experience firsthand the variety of flavors available for sale in the retail store.

JGA Southfield, MI

PROJECT DESIGN TEAM
Lori Robinson VP Corporate Branding & Communications
Kathleen Haley Director Corporate Branding & Communication

RETAIL DESIGN TEAM
Ken Nisch Chairman; Project Principal
Mike McCahill Project Manager
Jeff Clark Senior Designer

CLIENT
McCormick & Company/Sparks

ARCHITECT
JGA Southfield, MI

GENERAL CONTRACTOR
Builder Guru Contracting, Inc., Crofton, MD

OUTSIDE DESIGN CONSULTANTS
Bentz-Papson Associates *Retail Consultants*
Brand Theater LLC *Retail Consultants*
Lighting Management *Lighting Designer*

SUPPLIERS
EEI Global Rochester Hills, MI, *Fixtures/Millwork*

5th Screen Digital Services San Jose, CA, *Interactive Exhibits*
Blue Genie Art Austin TX, *Specialty/Theatrical Fixtures*
Triangle Sign Company Baltimore MD, *Signage*
Wilsonart Temple TX, *Laminates*
Sherwin Williams Cleveland, OH, *Paint*
CIOT Troy, MI, *Marble*

PHOTOGRAPHY
Laszlo Regos Photography Berkley, MI

Ann Summers

Westfield, Stratford City, London

SCOPE OF WORK Ann Summers offers lingerie and their signature collections of oils and lotions, "sexessories," novelties, and toys. According to the designers the brand had gone through a period of dramatic reinvention with a new positioning to "fearlessly unleash sexual confidence" at its heart. The retailer appointed FITCH to extend this striking new thinking to a new flagship store.

BRAND PROMISE The new store is a "playground for the curious," capturing the wit and glamour of the brand. Dramatic theatrical elements include double-height ceilings, and a flirtatious center stage for new products. A six-foot tall rabbit draws customers deeper into the store. The black, white and pink color palette, is both provocative and fun.

CUSTOMER JOURNEY Shoppers are taken on a journey from seduction and discovery to satisfaction—with the riskier products even placed in the center of the store. Meandering is encouraged, yet the products are presented with logical order. Apparel lines the walls, with a focal "stage" down the center. From the rotating tri-graphic window display, to the changing room keyhole entrance at the back of the store, the design creates moments of intrigue, and encourages customers to discover new products, and in turn, their own sexuality.

FIXTURING & FINISHES The fixture system helps to reduce clutter and bring focus to the product presentation. Making use of the double-height ceiling, some of the mannequins are placed on high shelves to create drama. The gloss black frames the fascia, contrasting with pink neon around the exterior, angled glass and the mirrored rotating tri-panels in the windows. Lavish materials such as the velvet rabbit and silk lampshade add to the sensuality.

LIGHTING Lighting creates drama for this playground. Spotlights highlight key collections yet leave shadows to encourage intimacy. Pink neon signage on the back wall draws people through the store and lighting behind the logo seductively pulsates in different colors.

VISUAL MERCHANDISING A multi-tiered "stage" down the center of the store showcases the latest products and collections. Jars and cake stands used as props heighten the link between food and sex. A "sexessories" wall presents smaller products and cross-merchandising. The visual merchandising strategy naturally guides people and allows them to meander through the space to encourage exploration.

GOALS ACHIEVED As the physical expression of the brand, the new store provides a fun, sexually-charged experience in an open and down-to-earth way. It showcases the product and encourages people to confidently explore and enjoy. With sales eight percent higher than expected, the regional manager describes the store as his crowning glory.

FITCH London

PROJECT DESIGN TEAM
For Ann Summers:
Fiona Davis Marketing Director;
Becki Rowe General Manager of Marketing

RETAIL DESIGN TEAM
For FITCH:
Michelle Hardy Design Director
Eleanor Holton Senior Designer
Elise Rowland Senior Designer
Debbie Dickens Senior Designer
Shaadee Alam Designer
Charlotte Harrison Designer

GENERAL CONTRACTOR
Heartbeat Redditch, Worcestershire

OUTSIDE DESIGN CONSULTANTS
PPS Shopfitters Ltd Northampton, UK

SUPPLIERS
Heartbeat Redditch, Worcestershire, UK, *Audio/Visual*
Heartbeat Redditch, Worcestershire, UK, *Ceilings*
Visplay Islington, London, *Fixtures*

Domus Tiles Ltd. West Molesey, Surrey, UK, *Flooring*
Grestec Tiles Ltd. Headcorn, Kent, UK, *Flooring*
Twentytwentyone London, *Furniture: Modus PLC chair and Knoll Saarinen chair*
Architonic Zurich, *Furniture: Schonbuch Collect bench and Thonet chair*
Niche Modern Beacon, NY, *Lighting: Binary Pendant*
Architonic Zurich, *Lighting: Blum Axo Light*
La Rosa Mannequins Milan, *Mannequins/Forms*
Prop Studios West Sussex, UK, *Props and Decoratives: Giant Rabbit*
Selfridges London, *Other props and decoratives*
Heywood Metal Finishers Huddersfield, West Yorkshire, *Wallcoverings and Materials*
Robert Horne Group Limited London, *Wallcoverings and Materials*
Lelievre London, *Wallcoverings and Materials*
Chase Erwin London, *Wallcoverings and Materials*
Chelsea Artisans London, *Wallcoverings and Materials*
Slough England, *Dulux /ICI Paints*

PHOTOGRAPHY
Jon Mead London, UK

Joe Fresh
NYC Flagship, 5th Avenue, New York, NY

SCOPE OF WORK Joe Fresh, Canada's home-grown fast-fashion retailer, enlisted the designers at Burdifilek to create the retailer's New York City Flagship property at the corner of 5th Avenue and 43rd Street. The 14,000 square-foot store occupies the historic Crystal Lantern, a landmark and modernist masterpiece designed by Skidmore, Owings and Merrill that was originally a bank. The new design was conceived to broaden the retailer's reach and strengthen the brand's presence in New York City and the United States. Reflecting Joe Fresh's approach to fashion, the store design is confident yet understated, with subtle and sophisticated nuances that create interest and distinguish the Joe Fresh aesthetic.

BRAND PROMISE The Joe Fresh promise is to provide customers with stylish, fresh and affordable fashion. The Joe Fresh New York City flagship location is a prominent and accessible venue for the brand to offer an inspired collection of well-priced products in the competitive fast-fashion marketplace.

CUSTOMER JOURNEY The store interior was designed to create a sense of discovery for customers, by way of compartmentalized spaces which guide customers throughout the store. Custom-designed free-floating merchandising structures allow for the merchandising team to arrange vignettes as desired, offering customers something new to discover each time they visit the store.

LIGHTING The building's 27-foot-high glass windows allow for an abundance of natural light, adding to the airy quality of the interiors. The store's floating white terrazzo mezzanine features uniform light panels, giving the impression of a glowing ceiling. This design approach helps to channel views into the store and upwards towards the glowing mezzanine and creates the impression of weightless architecture. Recessed pot-lights in the ceiling allow for directional merchandise lighting.

STORE PLANNING The designers kept the store open to the spectacular backdrop of the New York City streetscape, embracing the building's architectural bones and remaining open to its surroundings.

VISUAL MERCHANDISING The designer's intent was to create a sophisticated backdrop to showcase the Joe Fresh collection. Reflecting the brand's approach to fashion, careful attention was paid to subtle nuances that create interest and distinguish the brand aesthetic. Airy, colorful, urban and ever-changing, the store design underscores the Joe Fresh brand. Free-floating wardrobes can be easily arranged and reconfigured into vignettes to separate store sections and define specific collections as desired.

FIXTURING & FINISHES To protect the historic building, no shop fittings were drilled to the floor, walls or ceiling. Instead, free-floating merchandising systems complement the lightness of the host building. These custom-designed wardrobes can easily be arranged into vignettes to compose a different color story of clothing and accessories. The store's custom-designed wardrobes were crafted from white powder-coated metal with sand-blasted Lexan panels to transmit light. Display tables are powder-coated aluminum Parsons tables with benches, and white poly-carbonate cubes were poured from wood molds so that they have the texture of wood grain and the appearance of porcelain.

ENVIRONMENTAL GRAPHICS The Flagship's sculptural elements, such as a 70-foot-long gilded screen and a whimsical hanging "cloud mobile" by modernist sculptor and furniture designer Harry Bertoia, are a creative point of reference for shoppers, and act as visual touch points within the space.

ENVIRONMENTAL GRAPHICS The store design incorporates seamless monitors, mirrors and backlit billboards, along with a select number of glowing light boxes in Joe Fresh's signature orange with video screens displaying contemporary videos. These elements guide customers throughout the space, contribute to the liveliness of the space and allow the merchandise to glow. Contributing to the liveliness of the store and allowing the focus to remain on the merchandise and the Joe Fresh brand are dynamic monitors, back-lit billboards, glowing light boxes in the retailer's signature orange, and video screens displaying multimedia messages.

Burdifilek Toronto, ON

PROJECT DESIGN TEAM
Diego Burdi Design Director
Paul Filek Managing Partner
Jeremy Mendonca Senior Designer
Jacky Kwong Designer
Daniel Mei CADD
Edwin Reyes CADD
Anna Nomerovsky CADD
Anthony Tey CADD
Daniela Cerchie CADD
Tom Yip Project Manager

CLIENT
Joe Mimran Associates / Loblaws Inc.

ARCHITECT
Callison New York, NY, *Consulting Architect*
Skidmore Owings & Merrill LLP New York, NY, *Base Building Architect*

GENERAL CONTRACTOR
Richter+Ratner New York, NY

OUTSIDE DESIGN CONSULTANTS
Fiskaa Engineering New York, NY, *Consulting Engineer (Electrical, Mechanical)*
Highland Associates New York, NY, *Engineering*
Lighting Workshop New York, NY, *Lighting Consultant*

Archetype Consultants Inc. New York, NY, *Filing Agent/Code/Landmark Consultant*
Construction Planning Solutions *Project Management*

PHOTOGRAPHY
Ben Rahn, A-Frame Studio, Toronto, ON

Chicago Sports Depot
Chicago, IL

SCOPE OF WORK The goal was to create a sports destination flagship and entertainment venue that includes state-of-the-art technology and showcases the various Chicago teams, with the primary focus on the Chicago White Sox.

CUSTOMER JOURNEY The intended journey takes fans through a sensorial shopping experience that evokes an emotional connection to the teams and their legendary journeys to championships, leading to hometown pride and ultimately sales.

BRANDING Infused with an overall baseball theme, the store honors the Chicago White Sox with bigger than life murals while it celebrates and emotionally connects fans with the City of Chicago and its sports championships. Along with Sox merchandise the store features branded shop-in-shops for the Bears, Blackhawks and Bulls for an all-inclusive sports shopping experience.

ENVIRONMENTAL GRAPHICS Multi-story graphic focal areas are utilized to bring a sense of drama and create an experience akin to that of a championship game. Bigger than life championship mu-rals, featuring current and former players from the White Sox and other Chicago teams, brand the space with championship pride.

STORE PLANNING The environmental design incorporates a baseball stitching pattern on the floor that leads customers through the different team shops. The floor design also defines categories of merchandise, reinforces implied aisles, and moves fans and customers through the space using a dramatic, graphic approach.

VISUAL MERCHANDISING Operational ease of set-up and change-out are provided by flexible fixture designs that offer different configurations, enhancing the merchandising presentation and giving the products a stage to become the hero of this game.

GOALS ACHIEVED Given the challenges multi-level stores represent for retailers, one of the main goals of the project was to create an effective customer flow through the two-level space. A signature, LED video staircase captivates customers with an impressive digital branding statement while enticing them to shop both levels. More than 75 video monitors provide "infotainment" opportunities, including four feature video walls strategically positioned to help tell the story of the Chicago White Sox and show video feeds from live games and other entertainment programming.

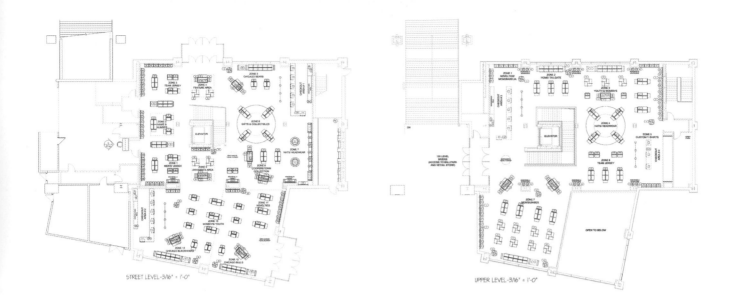

STREET LEVEL-3/16" = 1'-0"   UPPER LEVEL-3/16" = 1'-0"

FIXTURING & FINISHES A welcoming, easy-to-shop atmosphere is established through the mixture of customized fixtures and furniture that showcases collectibles and highlights key merchandise and memorabilia. Autographed collectibles are featured in memorabilia cases designed to be autographed themselves, bringing a touch of authenticity to the environment. Warm wood tones contrast with surrounding bold visual elements and bringing an eclectic and energizing feel to the store. Bold use of color and texture, video and large format graphics at the cash/wraps create a major brand presentation that anchors the space with Chicago White Sox heritage and fan appeal.

RGLA Solutions, Inc. Schiller Park, IL

PROJECT DESIGN TEAM
Robert Arend RGLA, Chief Operating Officer/Principal
Joseph Geoghegan Jr. RGLA, Chief Architectural Officer/Principal
Randy Sattler RGLA Chief Creative Officer/Principal
Sandi Leamon RGLA, Program Director/Sr. Architect
Jeff Stompor RGLA, Director of Design
Ivelisse Ruiz RGLA, Director of Brand Marketing
Melissa Watkins RGLA, Project Designer
Bill Dodge RGLA, Project Designer

RETAIL DESIGN TEAM
Jeff Hess DNC Sportservice Vice President of Retail

Roy Olsen Director Facilities Project Management
Joey Nigro General Manager, Sportservice, US Cellular Field

CLIENT
Delaware North Companies, Buffalo, NY

ARCHITECT
RGLA Solutions, Inc. Chicago, IL

GENERAL CONTRACTOR
James McHugh Construction Co. Chicago, IL

OUTSIDE DESIGN CONSULTANTS
Philips Lightolier *Overall Lighting*
Peter Basso Associates, Inc. *Specialty Lighting Consultant*
Philips Color Kinectics *LED Staircase*
Vision Integrated Graphics/Point Imaging *Graphics*

PHOTOGRAPHY
Charlie Mayer, Oak Park, IL

PEZ Visitor Center

Orange, CT

SCOPE OF WORK The overall design objective of the PEZ Visitor Center was to showcase PEZ as a fun interactive candy to devotees of the brand as well as to introduce the brand to a new generation of fans through a unique, engaging and entertaining venue. The new shopping destination offers a complete brand immersion into all things PEZ, from precious collectibles to fun and interactive games and trivia for kids—and kids at heart.

CUSTOMER JOURNEY The intended customer journey was to take visitors from the nostalgic beginnings of the PEZ brand to its current brand positioning in a lively and entertaining fashion. The space features the world's largest PEZ dispenser, a viewing area into the production factory, PEZ trivia games and an interactive historical timeline.

BRANDING The environment uses layered graphic elements that deliver the PEZ experience via colorful displays, theatrical fixtures, messages and collections throughout the space representing the brand from its vintage times to the present.

ENVIRONMENTAL GRAPHICS The color scheme is derived from the bright colors of the PEZ candy packaging, as well as the pastel colors of the PEZ candy tablets, injecting fun accents and energy into the space. Stripes of red, yellow and orange found on the signature PEZ Assorted Candy packaging are used to establish an iconic element for architectural structures, graphics and signage, fixtures and furnishings, unifying the environment with the brand.

STORE PLANNING The two story greeting area and "Wall of PEZ" welcomes visitors. Arches, vitrines and vaults are placed around the space to create a sense of discovery as they form a path to draw visitors through the experience. The retail area continues the theme of discovery while organizing the products into easy-to-shop categories. Licensed product are showcased on end caps with high impact graphics.

FIXTURING & FINISHINGS The World's Largest PEZ Dispenser welcomes visitors and celebrates the product. The arches encompass the community area and showcase the collection into smaller, focused presentations. The Wall of PEZ communicates the scope of the brand's influence and reach while the use of themed fixtures such as the vault-like showcase makes valuable collectibles stand out. Colorful vitrines are made out of lightweight foam and packaging-shaped benches and tablet-shaped ottomans utilize high density foam for comfort and longevity. Every color and finish selection is a representation of the brand.

VISUAL MERCHANDISING Custom exhibit fixturing conveys the attitude of the brand through color, texture and theatrical expression. The Wall of PEZ, The World's Largest PEZ Dispenser, and the Collectors' Community Arch Structure and Display Vitrines establish the iconic elements for the venue, taking cues from the brand's colorful packaging.

GOALS ACHIEVED More than 4,000 square feet was added to the headquarters to showcase the brand in a museum-like shopping environment offering the most comprehensive collection of PEZ memorabilia, games, factory tours and unique merchandise.

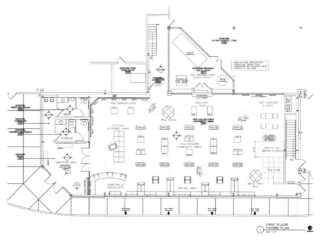

RGLA Solutions, Inc. Schiller Park, IL

PROJECT DESIGN TEAM
Robert Arend RGLA, Chief Operating Officer/Principal
Joseph Geoghegan Jr. RGLA, Chief Architectural Officer/Principal
Randy Sattler RGLA Chief Creative Officer/Principal
Sandi Leamon RGLA, Program Director/Sr. Architect
Jeff Stompor RGLA, Director of Design
Ivelisse Ruiz RGLA, Director of Brand Marketing
Melissa Watkins RGLA, Project Designer
Bill Dodge RGLA, Project Designer

RETAIL DESIGN TEAM
Joseph Vittoria CEO (PEZ Candy Inc., USA)
Keith Whitaker VP Marketing & Sales Administration (PEZ Candy Inc., USA)

Shawn Peterson Project Manager (PEZ Candy Inc., USA)

CLIENT
PEZ Candy Inc, USA

INTERIOR ARCHITECT
RGLA Solutions, Inc. Chicago, IL

GENERAL CONTRACTOR
Taulman Construction

OUTSIDE DESIGN CONSULTANTS
Arlotta Manchester Center, VT
Vision Integrated Graphics/Point Imaging
Blue Genie Art Industries

SUPPLIERS
Opto International Inc. Wheeling, IL, *Fixtures*
Specialty Woodworking Bedford Park, IL, *Millwork*
KMDI MicroLite Kansas City, KS, *Arches*
Madjek Amityville, NY *Exterior, Vitrines*
Kieffer Signs Mokena, IL, *Signage*

PHOTOGRAPHY
Ed Thomas Photography, Glastonbury, CT

CityTarget National Strategy

Multiple Urban Locations

SCOPE OF WORK Target's concept for CityTarget is to bring urban guests an exceptional one-stop shopping experience. By the end of 2013 the retailer will have CityTarget locations in Chicago, Seattle, Los Angeles, San Francisco and Portland.

BRAND PROMISE CityTarget stores are conveniently located for urban guests many of whom previously had to travel outside the city to visit a Target store. Commuters also enjoy the convenience of having CityTarget stores near their places of business. CityTarget's edited merchandise assortment offers a selection of apparel, accessories and home design products, as well as household basics, commodities and items suited for urban lifestyles.

STORE PLANNING Target's innovative approach to development and store design allows it to customize a distinctly Target experience for each unique CityTarget location.

Target Store Design Minneapolis, MN

PROJECT DESIGN TEAM
Sarah Amundsen, Director, Store Planning

ARCHITECT
Richard Varda, FAIA, Senior Vice President, Store Design

MARKETING
Todd Marshall, Senior Vice President, Marketing

PHOTOGRAPHY
Mark Steele Photography, Columbus, Ohio

I-Stick Store

Sao Paulo, Brazil

SCOPE OF WORK The designer Mauricio Queiroz was asked to create a concept for the first store for the I-Stick brand. The challenge was to develop a consistent and interesting visual connection between the store and the products—a uniform language that would unite store and product in the consumer's mind.

CUSTOMER JOURNEY I-Stick offers various home-related products that consumers can take home and "stick" to their walls and furnishings. Included are wall stickers, wallpaper, gadget "skins" and home accessories such as magazine racks and light fixtures— all brightly colored and patterned. The design had to encourage shoppers to explore the products and discover items they didn't even realize they needed. Suggestions as to the many places the sticky products can be stuck abound.

STORE PLANNING The open storefront invites shoppers to wander into the small space. The store, and the uniqueness of the brand can be seen at a glance, but further exploration yields rich rewards to the shopper. The red and white color scheme of the logo and packaging is carried throughout the store. Instead of a window display up front, the designers placed an open, lifted display at the rear of the store, a solution generated to make the customer feel inside the store while still in the hallway.

BRANDING The new design evolves the versatility for which the brand is known and renews the mix of products. A vast world of ideas is presented to the shopper—ideas that enrich their own home environments.

GOALS ACHIEVED The focus of the new design is on the products and the in-store learning experience provided to shoppers as they explore the product possibilities. The space is highly functional and allows effective consumer service. The resulting I-Stick store recognizes freedom of creativity and expression.

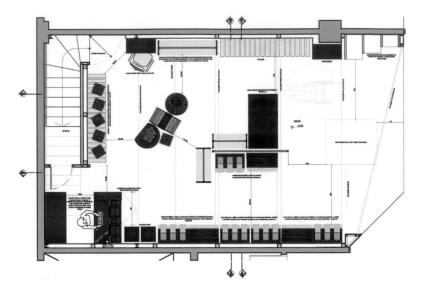

FIXTURING & FINISHES The utilization of every inch of space is of prime importance and the modular fixtures and shelving maximizes display area and provides flexibility. Materials are consistent with the modern brand image: concrete floor, metallic materials and "painting out" the ceiling elements with black.

Mauricio Queiroz Arquitetura Sao Paulo, Brazil

DESIGN/ARCHITECTURE TEAM
Mauricio Queiroz
Daniel Gouvea
Ana Carolina Frutuoso
Vitor Zonderico
Mônica Marinho
Tatiana Tortorelli

CLIENT
Elisa Rosa

GENERAL CONTRACTOR
Construtora Bonadia Sao Paulo, Brazil

SUPPLIERS
TRUST Technical Lighting *Lighting*
Ravena *Furniture*

PHOTOGRAPHER
Marco Antonio da Silva

Ole' supermarket G4
Chengdu, China

SCOPE OF WORK The objective was to build on the existing Ole' format — also created by the rkd retail/iQ — to develop the next generation G4 Ole' supermarkets with an enhanced category definition and expanded merchandise assortment.

BRAND PROMISE The first entrance for Ole' in western China, and within the most upscale shopping center in Chengdu, Ole' G4 delivers the highest level of customer service and the largest assortment of local and imported merchandise within a clear and contemporary environment that promotes an experience, exposure and choice. The design is the exact expression of the brand promise in terms of clarity of planning, interior design, graphic communications, category adjacencies, merchandise presentation/assortment and customer service.

ENVIRONMENTAL GRAPHICS From the entrance branding through to the price tags, the entire graphic program is unified through color, material and character to maintain a consistent communication story that is focused on information and benefits first, and price and promotion second.

LIGHTING Simple and straightforward general illumination of T5 florescent lighting is punctuated with flexible CDMT spotlights for highlighting and focus.

VISUAL MERCHANDISING Visual merchandising is directed at the product level in all categories of dry grocery, fresh food, housewares with a focus on clarity of offer, origin and product benefit.

STORE PLANNING Wide aisles and clear vistas to important focal elements create landmarks allowing customers to fulfill their weekly, or daily, shopping needs. Within the complete merchandise assortment and logical category adjacency there are various paths, or journeys, provided for the shopper. Beyond the basic supermarket gondolas—that are enhanced with special functions and materials—special fixtures were created in wood tones and framed and supported with dark metal accents.

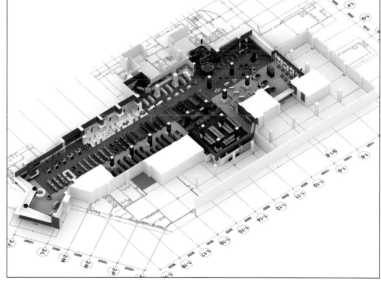

rkd retail/iQ Bangkok, Thailand

PROJECT DESIGN TEAM
RKurt Durrant Principal in Charge
Rungroj Chinbunchorn Creative Director
Chotima Chundprasit Interior Designer
Lalida Jirapachonpong Interior Designer
Torsak Surasaksilp Creative Director Graphics
Chusak Ornglaor Senior Graphic Designer
Sura Vetchasat Senior DDI
Narumon Samart Senior DDI
Thawatchai Tiemjarat Head CG/3D
Ada He Managing Director, rkd retail/iQ Shenzhen
Jade Deng Project Coordinator

RETAIL DESIGN TEAM
China Resources Vanguard Co Ltd
Long Chen Deputy Chairman and CEO
Hong Jie CEO
Qin Dong Sheng VP
Kevin Chen VP
Dai Hong GM of Business Department. Ole' CRV
Ou Xueqing Director of Standards Department. Ole' CRV

CLIENT
China Resources Vanguard, Shenzhen, China

GENERAL CONTRACTOR
Shenzhen Feifan Decoration Construction Design Ltd.

PHOTOGRAPHY
Pruk Dejkhamhaeng, Bangkok, Thailand

Longo's Leaside

Toronto, ON, Canada

SCOPE OF WORK The designers at Watt International were tasked by regional grocer Longo's with the development of a flagship shopping destination in a turn-of-the-century building that once was a locomotive repair shop. The design included all interior and exterior treatments, store planning, fixture design, merchandising concepts and in-store communications.

BRAND PROMISE Longo's focus on creating "fresh traditions" is consistent with the building. The environment reflects the retailer's respect for history, tradition and craft while providing moments of modern inspiration—critical to keeping the brand young and vital. The Longo family's own history in the food business is a story told throughout the store experience, further reinforcing the authenticity of their brand. From the identity graphics to every piece of furniture, the design pays homage to the past while embracing the future.

CUSTOMER JOURNEY The journey begins outside of the building with modern, solar lighting and parking for electric cars, setting a tone and creating a contrast with the historic brick building. On entry, the customer is met with an array of sensory inspiration—from the beautifully merchandised wine selection in the glass encased wine shop, to the sights and scents emanating from the kitchen where high quality ingredients are made into seductive cre-

ations. Customers can indulge in a light snack in Corks Wine Bar before continuing their grocery shopping.

FIXTURING & FINISHES Clear hierarchies are established to ensure that focus is always as intended and a topography of fixtures is used to draw customers into spaces. To bridge the established Longo's look and the historical elements of the site the designers developed a blend of warm dark colors and woods contrasted with crisp whites and vibrant, youthful colors. Architectural elements, including massive doors, are incorporated into walls and details.

LIGHTING Daylight enters through clerestory refitted with energy efficient, sealed double glazed units. Lower than typical light levels are supported with lighting placed closer to product. Enormous feature chandeliers, inspired by rail architecture, give warmth and intimacy to the soaring ceilings.

SUSTAINABILITY Solar lighting, electric car parking, sealed, double glazed windows, reclaimed wood tables and bar, re-used building elements, lead paint and other hazardous material abatement and closed refrigeration cases are among the many efforts made on this 100-year-old adaptive re-use of a site.

ENVIRONMENTAL GRAPHICS The standard graphic package employed in the rest of the chain was tailored to reflect the unique character of the site. Illustrations and graphic styles inspired by the period of the architecture are seamlessly integrated within a package that injects equal amounts of fresh color and contemporary graphic treatment. Forty-foot ceiling heights are exploited as moments of release at the beginning and end of the shop.

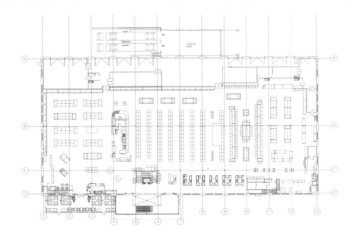

VISUAL MERCHANDISING Visual merchandising places focus clearly on product, with strategies configured to maximize the inspirational and appetite appeal of the merchandise, highlight service functions, and elevate customer engagement. Dark colors ensure that product is what is seen above all else, especially in fresh perishable areas.

GOALS ACHIEVED The store has drawn extremely positive reviews from media, local heritage authorities and customers. Results have exceeded plan by a significant margin since opening, and the warm and relaxed environment of Corks Wine and Beer Bar is becoming a community meeting place. Customers appreciate the attention to detail that is demonstrated by both the environment and merchandise.

Watt International Inc. Toronto, ON

PROJECT/RETAIL DESIGN TEAM
Tim Klein
Ash Pabani
Sienna Skelton
Sam Chan
Glen Kerr
Jean-Paul Morresi
Kathy Gorman
Ian Cooke

CLIENT
Longo Brothers Fruit Markets, Vaughan, ON

ARCHITECT
Scoler & Lee Architects Toronto, ON

GENERAL CONTRACTOR
Rochon Building Corp. Toronto, ON

OUTSIDE DESIGN CONSULTANTS
Neelands Refrigeration Limited *Layout and Refrigeration*
Cooper Lighting *Lighting*
Nelson & Garrett Lighting *Lighting (chandeliers)*
Hammerschlag & Jeffe Inc. *Lighting (layout)*
Hua Chen *HVAC*

SUPPLIERS
Armstrong Metal Clg Toronto, ON
CBSF, Canada's Best Store Fixtures Toronto, ON
    Signature fixtures/gondolas
Canadian Sign Systems Port Perry, ON
O'Connell Store Fixtures Inc. Toronto, ON
Chair Source Concord, ON,
Momentum Group Mississauga, ON
Tusch Seating Toronto, ON
Olympia Tile Toronto, ON

Pionite Toronto, ON
Nevamar Toronto, ON
Arborite Toronto, ON
Formica Toronto, ON
Olympla Wall Tile Toronto, ON
Vitroceram Toronto, ON
Benjamin Moore Toronto, ON
Cultured Stone Toronto, ON
Caesar Stone Toronto, ON
Option 3 display Montreal, QB
Dupont Zodiaq
Metro Concord, ON
Franklin Empire Toronto, ON

PHOTOGRAPHY
Release Credit Neil Hill, Toronto, ON

The Parlour

Seoul, Korea

SCOPE OF WORK Located in the basement of the headquarters of SPC Corporation—South Korea's largest restaurant chain operator— is The Parlour, a one-of-a-kind restaurant that has become the place to be seen among Seoul's fashionista set and business high flyers. The Parlour was born from an idea for a "bite-size boutique" that developed between the client and JHP, and in response to the lack in Korea of a "tea-room." The design agency was charged with bringing the whole experience to life, including the store concept, name generation, identity, graphics, visual merchandising, uniforms, menus, packaging, and service style.

BRAND PROMISE JHP developed four cornerstone values—*indulgence, feminine, artistic* and *luxury*—upon which they designed the concept. All work on the brand identity, the interior and the experience was to give The Parlour a timeless elegance and have it steeped in femininity, authenticity and quality. The brand's tone of voice is classic in its use of typeface and style. In-store graphics, menus, packaging and music all exude glamour and sophistication.

CUSTOMER JOURNEY Oriented towards women, this all-day destination operates as a coffee stop in the morning, a destination spot for lunch, a place to enjoy canapés and cakes during the afternoon tea slot, and culminates in a venue for champagne, cocktails and desserts at night. Luxurious, refined and elegant, the interior is designed around a sequence of seated spaces and snugs to accommodate varying groups of customers and needs.

STORE PLANNING The designers' major challenge was to drive footfall from the street, so the staircase was reconfigured and the entrance made as inviting as possible. The glamorous staircase is elegantly illuminated, right down to the storefront, with a beautiful exterior chandelier light feature overhead. The spaces and seating arrangements are defined by the customers' needs. Patrons can be served "grab and go" at counters or choose to dine at either the banquette seating on the perimeter or the raised banquette in the heart of the restaurant. Those wishing to leisurely linger can be seated in more relaxed café style seating or in an intimate snug.

ENVIRONMENTAL GRAPHICS As the storefront is in a recessed well in the void of the basement, the designers created a discrete lectern to showcase the menu at the top of the staircase. Just one glance down the illuminated stairwell, also lit with exterior candles, is enough to encourage customers to visit.

LIGHTING The intent of the lighting strategy is romance—suitably moody in places and not overly bright, while the design of the chandeliers is dramatic and indulgent. The lighting also changes to suit the restaurant's operation throughout the day.

VISUAL MERCHANDISING At The Parlour food presentation is treated with the same care as high-end boutiques treat this season's must-have fashions. Displayed with flair and panache, the delicate and dainty products are arranged on shelves and on plates, making the entire experience a lesson in expert product selection and display.

FIXTURING & FINISHES JHP designed counters in the form of traditional French country tables with white marble tops. All furniture was sourced from Europe and includes an eclectic mix of traditionally upholstered timber frame furniture and modern pieces. Antique elements such as cake trolleys, silver tea pots and dessert trays ensure that the experience is as authentic as it is luxurious. Hand blown glass pendant lamps hang above the counters. The snug features white herringbone wood block flooring, *objets d'art* and patterned wallpaper. High quality white marble is used for the flooring, and white polished plaster covers the walls. Fashion photography and illustrations adorn The Parlour's rooms and public spaces.

GOALS ACHIEVED According to the designers, customers instantly fell in love with The Parlour. The client received very positive feedback on the quality of the food, the service and the interior experience. The restaurant also gained lots of coverage in the Asian press. The space has been used for fashion and product launches and as a glamorous meeting venue—exactly what the designers set out to achieve.

JHP London

PROJECT DESIGN TEAM
Steve Collis Joint Managing Director
Raj Wilkinson Joint Managing Director
Darren Scott Creative Director
David Rook Director of Retail Design
Lucy Dyke Retail Designer

RETAIL DESIGN TEAM
JHP

CLIENT
SPC Corporation

GENERAL CONTRACTOR
SPC Corporation, internal construction company

PHOTOGRAPHY
Hee Won Cho, Seoul, South Korea

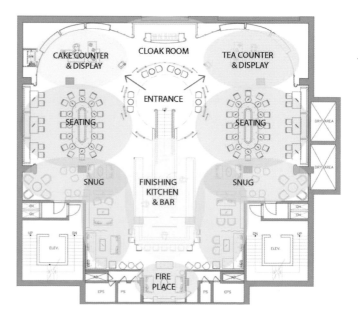

Hambar

Montreal, QC, Canada

SCOPE OF WORK The new Hambar management team decided to completely transform the former Vauvert restaurant on the ground level of the hip Hotel Saint-Paul in Montreal's old city, known as Old Montreal. The restaurant has a new identity, new menu and new look. The design mission was to shed the gloominess of the previous restaurant design and introduce a sparkling white, glamorous space; a trendy and casual spot where specialty cured meats are the stars of the show.

BRANDING The restaurant delivers a tongue-in-cheek sense of humour with its in-your-face entrance statement. Upon entering Hambar, patrons are greeted by a full-height showcase of theatrically-lit, suspended cured meats—the restaurant's epicurean specialty. The display, not normally found front and center at a restaurant, sends the message to customers that they have arrived at an iconoclastic establishment where nothing is sacred. The dichotomy of the lowly ham greeting visitors in an elegantly lit glass showcase more conducive for haute couture than raw meat, is a humorous take on the status of the pig and the restaurant's brand.

ENVIRONMENTAL GRAPHICS In keeping with the store's clean aesthetic, signage and graphics are minimal, however the beloved pig does figure throughout. The circular Hambar logo of a pig's head adorns all of the wine glasses, plates and printed graphics.

STORE PLANNING In order to increase the visibility of the activity within the restaurant to passersby, a raised platform was built for the tables to sit upon so both patrons and passersby can "see and be seen" through the atypically high windows. All built-ins from the former restaurant spanning the width of the window wall were removed and new full-height wood panels frame the windows, providing clear vistas onto Place d'Youville. The main bar unconventionally displays bottles on glass shelves fastened to a rough concrete wall with standards typically used for apparel merchandising. Again, an intentional wink saying, "As much as we can build our concept around a pig, we can also use display systems intended for different types of merchandise in our own signature way."

LIGHTING The recessed lighting within the ceiling trough above the communal table accentuates the length of the lively table. The pin lights suspended from flexible metal tubes in front of the mason wall add whimsy. The suspended chandeliers comprised of clusters of custom shaped light bulbs, inject the requisite dose of glam appeal. Recessed lighting along the window wall highlights the depth of the walnut grain of the full-height panels.

GOALS ACHIEVED The restaurant is a destination for diners seeking an animated and lively setting where they are guaranteed a highly specialized dining experience. It promises action, people-watching entertainment and refined food within a sleek yet unpretentious environment. Within a very short period of time, Hambar has become a very popular destination. Patrons do not recognize the restaurant in its new incarnation of its former self and relish the bustling convivial atmosphere, evocative of an upscale bistro.

CUSTOMER JOURNEY Customers can either sit at the oversized communal table in the middle of the restaurant, at the wood slab bar, or on the raised platform along the windows with a prime view of the charming town square. At the rear of the space directly opposite the main entrance, an imposing wine cellar sits next to a full-height wall of mason jars with marinades and pickling juices. The prominent meat slicing machines in front of the mason jar wall, coupled with the wine cellar, provide strong focal points. The charcuterie station is abuzz with frenetic activity as the on-site butcher tries to keep pace with the steady stream of orders.

FIXTURING & FINISHES The design of the restaurant strikes a balance between machismo and feminine glamorous touches. On the masculine side, dark leather seating, walnut paneling and plank flooring; and on the feminine side, sparkling clusters of lights emulating chandeliers, and crisp white walls.

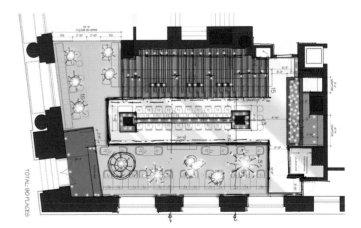

GH+A Montreal, QC

PROJECT DESIGN TEAM
Steve Sutton Partner
Guylaine Biron Project Director
Gabriel Dufresne Designer
Serge Prud'homme Senior Architectural Technologist
Evgueni Khalkov Architectural Technologist

CLIENT
Philippe Poitras, Montreal, QC

OUTSIDE DESIGN CONSULTANTS
Mercor Lighting Group *Lighting Consultants*
RAID *Brand Consultants for Logo*

SUPPLIERS
Atelier JR Sherbrooke, QC, *Millwork and Furniture*
Hermès Montreal, QC, *Chairs*
Corlite Montreal, QC, *Lighting supplier*
Union Lighting Montreal, QC, *Lighting supplier*

Ciot Montreal, QC, *Tiles*
Olympia Montreal, QC, *Tiles*
Formglas Toronto, ON, *Pre-fab Concrete Panels*
Renovatech Montreal, QC, *Custom Glass*

PHOTOGRAPHY
Yves Lefebvre, Montreal, QC

Happy's
Boston, MA

SCOPE OF WORK Renowned chef Michael Schlow collaborated for a third time with the designers to create his latest restaurant, Happy's, located next to Boston's fabled Fenway Park. The 4100 sq. ft. space incorporates a 32-table dining room, a 15-seat bar area with additional table seating, and an outdoor patio area. The scope of work included interior design and furniture selection.

BRAND PROMISE The Happy's promise is to provide cuisine that is a delicious take on American favorites, enjoyed in an ambiance as easy-going and friendly as your neighborhood bar. Schlow's mission is to offer a gourmet take on classic American comfort food in a casual atmosphere. The design celebrates Schlow's concept by crafting a hip but down-home hybrid—a witty, unpretentious space reflecting Happy's menu—part mom-and-pop diner, part "see and be seen" urban hot spot, part Sunday dinner at grandma's.

CUSTOMER JOURNEY The journey begins on the urban streetscape filled with friends, neighbors and fellow Red Sox fans. Once inside, customers can choose between the bar scene, a terrace, or the quieter, sit-down dining area. Whatever their choice, pa-trons are assured a relaxed experience and fare to please the most discerning diner.

ENVIRONMENTAL GRAPHICS Graffiti created by local artists is splashed across the walls, greeting patrons with an immediate blast of color, energy, and "street cred." The far wall of the bar area is filled with an oversized, kitschy print advertisement right out of the 1950s.

STORE PLANNING From the entry the bar is to the left with glass French doors opening onto the sidewalk patio. Straight ahead is the dining area. At the end of the dining room is an open kitchen. Long wooden chef's table are located in the space between diners and the kitchen area.

LIGHTING A mix of vintage chandeliers feels honky-tonk, Rosie-the-Riveter industrial, and retro chic. A custom chandelier over the reception desk at the entry is created from teacups and teaspoons. Black barrel lampshades with color interiors define the length of the bar.

GOALS ACHIEVED The design embodies the blend of American warmth, humor, and gourmet comfort food that Schlow envisioned. His mission was to offer a gourmet take on classic American comfort food in a warm, laid-back, familiar atmosphere. Mix-and-match tables, chairs, upholstered sofas, lamps, and armchairs evoke the funky flea market feel that is everyone's first apartment. Dining tables inscribed with buzz words, quirky artwork, tin ceilings, graffiti and a wall mosaic of hammered bottle caps created by local artists decorate the space. Happy's décor seems to have evolved over time with unlikely but somehow compatible elements from every decade since the 1930s. The atmosphere invites patrons to kick back, relax, and enjoy the great food and Grey Goose milkshakes that fuel the good times. As one patron described Happy's: "It's impossible to be sad in this place."

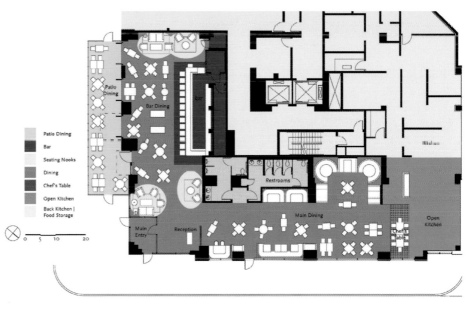

Elkus Manfredi Architects Boston, MA

PROJECT DESIGN TEAM
Elizabeth Lowrey
Marianne Weiss
Alina Wolhardt
Mark Naher

CLIENT
Good Essen, LLC, Boston, MA

ARCHITECT
Elkus Manfredi Architects Boston, MA

GENERAL CONTRACTOR
Cafco Construction Boston, MA

SUPPLIERS
Casa Design Boston, MA, *Furniture*
Furniture Concepts Woburn, MA, *Furniture*

SL Group Boston, MA, *Furniture*
Mohr & McPherson Boston, MA, *Furniture*
Cake Vintage Table & Home Nashville, TN, *Lighting*
Arteriors Carrolton, TX, *Lighting*
Cyan Design Ft. Worth, TX, *Lighting*
Threads Holliston, MA, *Drapery*
Bodega Boston, MA, *Artwork graffiti installation*
Mark Grundig Boston, MA, *Distressing of walls and stenciling*
Christina Zwart Boston, MA, *Bottle cap installation in bar area*

PHOTOGRAPHER
Mr. Jasper Sadidad San Francisco, CA

MyBurger Reinvention

Minneapolis, MN

SCOPE OF WORK When locally-owned, family-run MyBurger wanted to expand, FAME recommended an all-encompassing brand overhaul, from brand essence statement through identity, packaging, website and environmental design. The goal was to create a design-driven environment that established a template for all locations, but customizable enough to feel locally relevant to each location's clientele. The designers needed to offer something special that could roll out on a large scale, endearing the brand to consumers neighborhood by neighborhood. Since the goal was to create a sustainable model that supported MyBurger's expansion plan, a majority of the project's success would be measured by restaurant traffic and sales.

BRAND PROMISE Focus groups which included some of My-Burger's most loyal customers surprisingly revealed that food was not the primary driver. People loved the food, but they seemed far more excited when talking about their experience. The designers at FAME realized that the experience of visiting MyBurger needed to feel special—personal and locally connected. The new space needed to be a place where people want to linger and—more importantly—come back.

CUSTOMER JOURNEY From the street, the new identity, custom typography and vibrant palette established a retro-meets-modern brand that enabled MyBurger to stand out in a world of endless burger offerings. Inside, the designers leveraged warm wood tones and riveted concrete, while dimensional type brought the brand voice into the space. Elements of surprise such as local street names, stacked condiment jars with custom labels, a mustard-themed art installation, unexpected pops of color, and a vibrant mural near the back entrance added touches of humor and an intriguing layer of discovery everywhere customers looked.

STORE PLANNING To balance the customer experience with the kitchen and back-of-house requirements in this long, narrow space, functional areas are located along the interior wall, allowing dramatic views through industrial sized windows in the front and rear. Customers que from left to right, order, then go to the soda fountain and finally select seating.

LIGHTING The main interior wall is lit for street visibility, and also to highlight the sculptural graphic pieces on the walls. This created enough reflected ambience so the designers only supplemented with down lights in key areas. Vintage-modern-style pendants are positioned over tables, adding warmth to customer seating areas.

ENVIRONMENTAL GRAPHICS The designers infused the brand's voice into everything from permanent architectural elements to condiment jar labels. They used menu references, including retro-style custom-painted malt mixers, as a layer of discovery. Overhead architectural baffles add a neighborhood element, while a localized focal mural defines the back entrance. A single overhead menu board displays the burger offerings, along with sides, beverages, shakes and malts. It is visually clean and consistent with the environment, simplifying the offerings with branded headings such as "Kinda Fancy" or "Spiff it Up." On one wall are displayed limited edition T's and hats. Warm wood accents (floating shelves, focal walls, ceiling panels and tables) offer a nice counterpoint to the overall industrial vibe created by subway tile, riveted concrete walls, welded metal trays and powder-coated industrial chairs. Dimensional type, vibrant wall graphics and pops of color serve as focal points throughout the space.

BRANDING The designers at FAME determined the point of differentiation was all about the experience, they focused on ownable elements, from custom type, to original artwork, local references and an easy-modern environment. The unique brand voice and touches of humor in the illustrations and art installations bring humor and humanity to the experience. Playful "props" serve as branded installation art seamlessly connected to MyBurger offerings. Displays feature everything from retro-style malt mixers in brand colors, to stacked jars of condiments with custom labels. There is even a row of upside down mustard pours.

GOALS ACHIEVED According to the client the new design concept has established MyBurger as a local fast casual restaurant chain that is conceptually differentiated from the competition, poised for expansion and sustainable over time. With no budget for traditional advertising and mass awareness communications, the restaurant environment and experience needed to single-handedly create enough excitement and buzz with the neighborhood locals. The client is completely dependent on talk value, so the space and experience needed to wow consumers into becoming enthusiastic brand advocates. And it did. The new space invites, energizes and exudes authenticity while staying true to MyBurger's roots.

MYBURGER®

FAME Minneapolis, MN

PROJECT/RETAIL DESIGN TEAM
Bruce Edwards Chief Creative Officer
Nick Smasal Senior Designer
Conrad Chin Environmental Design Director
Julie Feyerer Creative Director, Copywriter

CLIENT
Paul & John Abdo

ARCHITECT
Hay Dobbs Minneapolis, MN

GENERAL CONTRACTOR
Zeeman Construction North Golden Valley, MN

SUPPLIERS
Lawrence Signs St. Paul, MN, *All outdoor and indoor signage/letters, etc.*

Minnefex Minneapolis, MN, *Specialty items: ketchup, mustard & pickle jars, mixers, colored bottles, upside down mustard bottles with spills, sandblasting and painting of colored chairs*
Archetype St. Paul, MN, *Magnetic/changeable menu board*
Industry West Jacksonville, FL, *Metal chair supplier*
BP Graphics Phoenix, AZ, *Printed and installed wall mural*
Aaron Carlson Minneapolis, MN, *Millwork*

PHOTOGRAPHER
Brian Droege Minneapolis, MN

Café Plenty
Toronto, ON, Canada

SCOPE OF WORK The designers at II By IV Design were asked to work within a narrow space of just over 900 sq. ft. and guide a novice owner on how best to showcase the product while balancing functional workspace with dining space.

GOALS ACHIEVED The goal was to showcase the product as simply as possible to be consistent with the ingredient-focused menu while building brand recognition. The designers accomplished this by using a white-on-white color scheme to keep focus on the product and using large acrylic signage and vinyl decals to reinforce name recognition.

BRAND PROMISE Having travelled throughout Europe researching and finding inspiration from different food cultures, the owner's product offerings includes well thought-out menu items that balance nutrition with sophisticated flavors in a refined but unpretentious atmosphere.

STORE PLANNING Circulation was a challenge. Without cluttering the small space with directive signage, the designers devised a traffic flow that is intuitive. Some clients are drawn immediately to the left to peruse what is on offer, while rushed clients are drawn to pre-packaged items in the fridge on the right. Separating the flow is a bar dining area.

FIXTURING & FINISHES Fixturing includes large, simple items such as counters with large glass screens housing various ceramic and metal trays, open fridges and reclaimed timber shelving. Mosaic floor and bevelled subway tiles are interrupted by bat and board wainscoting and accents of burnished brass, galvanized steel and reclaimed timbers. These accents add a slight mariner aesthetic without looking nautical.

LIGHTING Floor-to-ceiling windows at the entrance maximize natural light, while pot lights reflect off the white surfaces throughout. Wall mounted and hanging galvanized iron and brass fixtures highlight menu boards and counters.

VISUAL MERCHANDISING Products are showcased market-style in the open fridge or glass-topped counter in staggered elevations using varied ceramic, metal and wooden pedestals and trays.

CUSTOMER JOURNEY The customer feels relaxed in the approachable space which melds a fresh appeal with tactile natural finishes such as wood and copper. The ambience reflects the fact that the food is natural and as healthful as it looks. Keeping features proportional in the narrow space, food is exhibited in glass cases and fridges prominently placed near windows. The fresh appeal is rooted in a white-on-white color scheme mixed with tactile elements more common at a seacoast than a downtown core, giving the café a modern-rural air.

ENVIRONMENTAL GRAPHICS Large acrylic signage and vinyl decals on glass and mirror act to bolster the new brand's recognition. Wayfinding is natural as the line progresses down the narrow space from counter towards the cash register.

II BY IV DESIGN Toronto, ON

PROJECT DESIGN TEAM
Dan Menchions
Keith Rushbrook
Laura Abanil
Tracy Look Hong

CLIENT
Melissa Patterson, Toronto, ON

GENERAL CONTRACTOR
Anjinov Management Toronto, ON

SUPPLIERS
Eurolite Toronto, ON

Design Within Reach Toronto, ON
Circa Lighting
Brenlo Toronto, ON
Ciot Toronto, ON
Benjamin Moore Toronto, ON
Cercan Tile Toronto, ON
Silver Root Toronto, ON

PHOTOGRAPHER
David Whittaker Toronto, ON

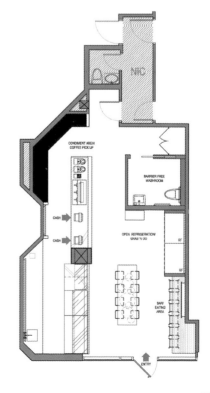

Suits Lobby Lounge

Trump International Hotel & Tower, Toronto, ON, Canada

SCOPE OF WORK The scope specified the creation of a bar that would extend from the lobby of a five-star hotel and carry through the hotel's aesthetics while becoming a destination in its own right, appealing to the local financial crowd and international guests.

BRAND PROMISE The brand promises its patrons an atmosphere of opulence and exclusivity, communicated by the dark palette of high-end finishes with limited seating. The designers delivered on this promise by utilizing the highest quality craftsmanship and materials to communicate an air of refinement.

ENVIRONMENTAL GRAPHICS Due to its small size, extensive wayfinding is not necessary. To counter the extravagant interior, entries are simple floor to ceiling clear glass portals. To highlight the location, a ticker tape announcing stock prices continually runs on the wall behind the bar.

STORE PLANNING Within the Lounge's diminutive frame, guests are ensconced as if in a jewelry box and discover intricate details in each well-chosen vignette. Circulation is done by the appraising eye.

FIXTURING & FINISHES Highlighting a well curated bar are antiqued Italian glass, sparkling Galaxy granite and brass fittings. The high-quality finishes impart a feeling on being part of an exclusive circle. Patterned granite flooring leads to macassar ebony panelling stretching the length of the bar topped with a Galaxy granite counter. Predominantly black and grey seating is offset by four striking gold chairs, which are reportedly always the first seats taken. A chandelier-like sculpture of crystals hangs above a communal table.

LIGHTING The lighting is dim and seductive. Tiny pot lights scatter reflections off glass and stone, and lighting hidden within valances softens shimmering gold sheers.

CUSTOMER JOURNEY A guest seated in one area of the lounge for their entire stay will enjoy a visual journey of textures, finishes and details that delight. From the obsidian-like chandelier and audacious gold chairs to mesmerizing Galaxy granite, Suits Lobby Lounge is a place to see and be seen.

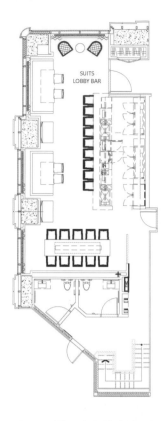

GOALS ACHIEVED The goal was to provide a very exclusive and upscale atmosphere within a small footprint that would appeal to the neighborhood financial crowd. The design of the bar is intentionally compact in reaction to the local taste for crowded after work drinks. The captivating sparkle of the impeccably detailed lounge conveys a message of opulence, and exclusivity.

II BY IV DESIGN Toronto, ON

PROJECT DESIGN TEAM
Dan Menchions
Keith Rushbrook
Ali Priestman
Adriana Mazzone
Peter Vandenberg
Thomas Moore
Vivian Wong
Ken Lam
Tracy Look Hong
Laura Abanil

CLIENT
Talon International Development Inc.

ARCHITECT
Zeidler Partnership Architects Toronto, ON

GENERAL CONTRACTOR
Lewis Builds Toronto, ON
Brookfield Multiplex Toronto, ON
B.L.T. Construction Services Inc. Toronto, ON

OUTSIDE DESIGN CONSULTANTS
Hidi Rae Consulting Engineers *Engineers*
    (AV, Electrical, Mechanical and Telecom)
Halcrow Yolles *Structural Engineers*
J.E. Coulter Associates Ltd. *Acoustical*
Randal Brown & Associates Ltd. *Code*
Orion Hardware *Hardware*
Trend Foodservice Design & Consulting *Kitchen*
IBI Group *Landscape*
OZZ Electric Inc. *Electrical*
Lisi Mechanical *Plumbing and Mechanical*
Vipond Inc. *Sprinklers*
Project 3 Sixty *Procurement*
Norm Li Architectural Graphics +
    Illustrations *Renderings*

SUPPLIERS
Benjamin Moore *Paint*
York Marble *Stone Floor and Bar Top*
NGI Designer Glass *Antique Mirror*
Louis Interiors *Upholstered Goods Including Banquette*
Mark David *Tables*
Metro Wall Covering *Wall Coverings*
Royal Lighting *Custom Light Fixture*
Valley Forge *Sheer Drapery*
Izzy Gallery *Framed Mirror*
The Art Shoppe *Consoles*
Ralph Lauren Home *Side Table at Window*

PHOTOGRAPHER
David Whittaker Toronto, ON

Urban Eatery at Toronto Eaton Centre

Toronto Eaton Centre, Toronto, ON, Canada

SCOPE OF WORK The Urban Eatery brings together the tenant space and seating area of what were previously two separate food courts located at opposite ends of the expansive shopping center. The relocated food court's mission is to be the ultimate casual urban dining experience within a classic modernist setting. The experience is differentiated by a tenant offering unique to the food court market that includes local Toronto restaurateurs in addition to national chains. The brand promise of the Urban Eatery is to provide an affordable, high quality and healthy fast-service dining option in the downtown core.

CUSTOMER JOURNEY A red signature wall in the main rotunda entrance on the ground level above the Urban Eatery acts as a beacon to incite hungry mall patrons to visit the food court below. A wide variety of seating styles and different zones offer visual breaks among the nearly one thousand seats. There are open spaces, communal tables, bar height tables and low seating granting the customers different experiences each time they visit.

BRANDING The Urban Eatery's signature element of downtown Toronto is represented as a stylized, red, city grid on lacquered panels. The branding strategy considered everything from the branding of all plates and glasses with the city grid pattern, to font types for menu display items, to food presentation and even staff uniforms.

FIXTURING & FINISHES Each tenant created a one-of-a-kind design for their brand that adhered to the principles outlined in the Design Criteria. All fixtures were designed in keeping with an urban

aesthetic, yet highly durable to withstand the rigors of one million visitors per week. A main corridor wall has been treated with acid edge blue mirror for contrast against all other high gloss white tile walls. High gloss metallic glazed porcelain mosaic tiles clad the low walls (bar counters) and the wall at elevator entrance. Columns are covered with faux concrete, fiberglass and stainless steel. Fixtures are all custom millwork and include long communal tables at bar height made from white quartz, stainless steel, colored resin and glass, and bar counters in resin, high gloss metallic porcelain tiles and stainless steel.

LIGHTING Major consideration was taken to create a restaurant ambiance in a subterranean environment. Recessed lights accentuate major architectural elements; LED colored accent lighting integrated in the bulkhead/coves delineates the center island zone and entrance at the escalators; Tom Dixon suspended polished chrome fixtures celebrate the classic '60s furniture in the seating niches.

SUSTAINABILITY The landlord of the property, Cadillac Fairview, is wholly committed to environmental protection through its "Green at Work" program. The program is responsible for significant reduction of waste and water consumption through the introduction of washable dishware and high efficiency equipment in the scullery. By relying on reusable dishware and state-of-the-art waste processing equipment, waste has virtually been eliminated and generates 50 tons of compost per year compared to the 400 tons of garbage previously sent to landfill.

VISUAL MERCHANDISING At over 60,000 sq. ft., a major challenge, the designers reported, was how not to make the food court feel like a voluminous hall with a sea of seats. The answer was varied seating layouts to support a dynamic customer experience and the creation of four freestanding island locations to promote a more interesting traffic flow, avoiding a typical "run of retailers." At the core of the Urban Eatery, the four island units are cohesively contained within a rectangular area of stainless steel finished columns, blue patterned glass and a suspended perimeter lighting fixture with at-counter diner style seating. The Urban Eatery raises the bar in terms of tenant design and presentation. Carefully crafted design criteria ensure that a singular vision is embraced by all tenants, resulting in a harmonious intermingling of national food chains and local restaurateurs. The leasing team solicited new-to-fast-food-market tenants from favorite local restaurants and coached them on how to convert their operations to a fast food format.

ENVIRONMENTAL GRAPHICS Clear glass demising partitions between tenants create transparency and open vistas in addition to signage opportunities. Strict criteria limiting the use of stainless steel with cut-out letters on the glass demising partitions promotes a unified expression of the various brands. Custom patterned glass serves as backdrops for island tenant signs. Graphics on all tenant menu boards, POP signs and supporting promotional material were individually reviewed and reworked until they met Design Committee approval.

GOALS ACHIEVED The space appeals to the target demographic groups of young urban multi-cultural students and residents, downtown office workers and tourists in a visual language that is hip and international. The food court reflects urbanism, multi-culturalism and the city of Toronto. Urbanism is reflected through the contemporary design cues, multi-culturalism through its ethnic food diversity, and the city of Toronto through the presence of some of the city's local casual restaurants, and the ever-present red city grid.

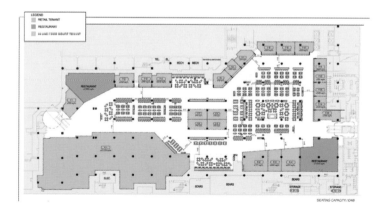

GH+A Montreal, QC

PROJECT DESIGN TEAM
Denis Gervais Partner
Joni Vallon Project Director
Philomène Poulin Senior Designer
Anne Cahsen Graphic Designer

CLIENT
Cadillac Fairview, Wayne Lee

ARCHITECT
Queens Quay Architects International Inc. Toronto, ON

GENERAL CONTRACTOR
PCL Construction Mississauga, ON

OUTSIDE DESIGN CONSULTANTS
Gabriel McKinnon Ottawa, ON, *Lighting Consultant*
Hidi Rae Consulting Engineers Inc. Toronto, ON, *Mechanical and Electrical Consultants*

SUPPLIERS
All Wood Fine Interiors LTD Toronto, ON *Millwork and Furniture; Custom metal*
Nelson and Garrett Toronto, ON, *Custom Lighting*
Cooper Lighting Mississauga, ON, *Lighting*
Nienkamper Toronto, ON, *Tom Dixon suspended accent lighting*
Excellent Signs and Displays, Inc. London, ON *Exterior Sign & LED*

Centura Montreal, QC, *Floor tiles*
Savoia Montreal, QC, *Wall tiles*
Ramacieri Soligo Montreal, QC, *Accent tiles*
GAB Montreal, QC, *3 form resin (counter and low wall)*
Accura Glass Bending Inc. Concord, ON, *Custom laminated glass & patterned glass (motif by GH+A)*
All Wood Fine Interiors LTD Toronto, ON, *Custom patterned mdf sculpted panels (motif by GH+A)*

PHOTOGRAPHER
Philip Castleton Toronto, ON

Jordan Flight Lab 2012
NBA All-Star Game, Miami, FL

SCOPE OF WORK The Jordan Brand needed a mobile pop-up shop for the three-day 2012 NBA All-Star Game. The shop introduced the new Air Jordan 2012 shoes to a variety of celebrity guests and fans who held special promotional tickets.

BRAND PROMISE The Jordan brand's reputation for high quality is bolstered by the use of materials and design, which communicates luxury and a streamlined contemporary street style. This combination of sport and style is the hallmark of the Jordan brand, and makes it sought after by elite players and fans alike.

CUSTOMER JOURNEY As customers approached the shop they were greeted by the Jordan "jump man" symbol and AJ2012 in white dimensional lettering against a black background. A brand ambassador greeted guests and ushered them through each stage of the process: "Choose Your Style," "Choose Your Ride," and "Choose Your Fit." Guests are educated about the different options available and the brand ambassador could accept payment through a mobile checkout system. The circulation was controlled by the linear format of the space and consumers were guided on a pathway through all of the rooms.

FIXTURING & FINISHES Guests were given their first look at the AJ2012 shoe at the top of the entry staircase, where a museum-like display case held a sample shoe on a pedestal. Infinity boxes displayed the shoes in every color combination from a multitude of angles. As customers exited the space, their final image was of a wall of shoe products surrounding the "jump man" symbol. Gleam-ing basketball hardwood floors and gloss black walls were utilized in the Flight Lab. The wall slats were at 23 degrees, a subtle nod to Michael Jordan's jersey number. Leather benches and black carpeting contrasted with multi-colored light boxes and laser-etched acrylic.

LIGHTING The feel of playing on an actual NBA court in a stadium was created in "Choose Your Style" with bright lighting on the floorboards, contrasting with the dark walls and ceilings above. Throughout the shop, high-contrast pin spots were utilized to enhance the theatrical experience, and back-lit acrylic panels glowed with information about each shoe variety.

VISUAL MERCHANDISING "One Shoe, Three Flights" was the theme of the shop. "Choose Your Ride" presented a visual decision tree for the consumer to piece together their dream shoe, which created a visually stunning tie-in with the product line. Guests chose from six colors, high- or low-top, and one of three insole styles, giving them three dozen possible combinations.

SALES TECHNOLOGY Technology provided a seamless customer experience. An iPad table educated the consumer with custom-programmed interactive software. Each brand ambassador carried an iPad that he or she used to enter customers' information and product selection, and assemblers in a back room received that information on their iPads. The overall effect was a seamless execution that satisfied customers' needs before they were even aware of them.

GOALS ACHIEVED The execution created a customer experience of a high-end retail environment within the confines of a pop-up shop. The designers custom-engineered two semi-trailers joined together side-by-side with collapsible walls and detailed connection docks, employed high gloss luxury finishes and materials throughout, and wired in dynamic lighting and backlit graphic effects to make the products shine.

LIT Workshop Portland, OR

PROJECT DESIGN TEAM
Damon Johnstun Creative Director
Liza Walsh Design Manager
Peter Morain Designer
John Pendleton Designer
Kyle Kendrick Designer
Mike Ryan Drafter

RETAIL DESIGN TEAM
Damon Johnstun Creative Director
Kirstin Kendall Account Executive

CLIENT
Brand Jordan, Beaverton, OR

ARCHITECT
Darren Palmer Portland, OR

GENERAL CONTRACTOR
Jon Hopmann, LIT Workshop Portland, OR

PHOTOGRAPHER
Dana Hoff Miami, FL

Sunglass Hut Floating Store
Campbells Cove, Sydney, Australia

SCOPE OF WORK The brief was to bring the Sunglass Hut brand to life in a dramatic and exaggerated way to allow re-connection with their customers in a cool and credible way. The client wanted an authentically exciting retail experience that was unique to Australian shoppers.

GOALS ACHIEVED To achieve this goal and activate the 2011 summer season, a bold and amplified brand experience was launched with the creation of a floating Sunglass Hut store on Sydney Harbour. The unique vessel, docked at Sydney's Darling Harbour, wowed customers with exclusive product offerings in a new and exciting store. The brand's promise to make available the latest, fashion-forward styles while maintaining a cool, fun and sexy attitude was fulfilled.

STORE PLANNING Sunglass Hut's circular logo was the inspiration for the shop's design. A radial steel structure formed the skeleton of the shop with dual curved, clear, acrylic panels located between each column to display the designer eyewear range.

FIXTURING & FINISHES The design blurred the line between internal and external. The curved acrylic display panels were secured with mirror-polished stainless steel spider fittings, and included sandblasted acrylic frame holders to give the sunglasses a floating effect. Only the very best high-end materials were used. Materials had to withstand 100° F+ temperatures in full sunlight, corrosive salt spray, driving rain, unpredictable wind gusts, and also the constant movement of the sea. Finishes were required that could transition seamlessly between the stylish interior of the shop to the grueling external marine environment.

LIGHTING The Floating Store was lit by a combination of natural sunlight and the latest generation of low power LED spotlights.

VISUAL MERCHANDISING To provide space for narrative a horizontal black storyboard was pinned off each acrylic display panel. This allowed hero products to be highlighted. In addition, vertical mirrors were used to transition the space between each display panel, along with matching vertical sparkle panels externally. The Central Display consisted of lockable "Butler" finished Go Go Units each displaying one piece of exclusive stock.

CUSTOMER JOURNEY The customer was enticed aboard by not only the unique style of the store, but also by the world-premiere sunglass styles that were not available to the general public until three months after the event. A DJ, located at the front of the shop created a fun party atmosphere and a sense of theater to the event. The customer, once on board, was greeted by Sunglass Hut associates from all over the world, chosen for their outstanding customer service. Customers could choose to be guided around the circular retail space or explore it for themselves.

SUSTAINABILITY The Floating Store was designed in a modular way so that it could be disassembled and stored in a shipping container for later use. Designed with sustainability in mind, the main structure was made of easily recyclable structural steel beams.

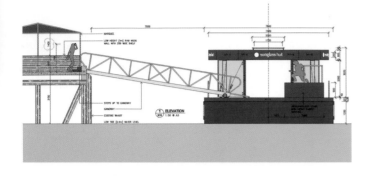

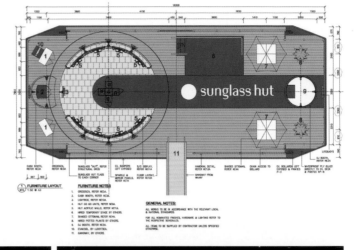

BRANDING The objective was to bring genuine excitement to the shopping experience. By removing the traditional four walls of a store and substituting the beautiful Sydney Harbor, the designers amplified the shopping experience to a new level. The sound of lapping water and myriad commercial vessels moving in the background added to the excitement. A DJ booth and lounges to the rear of the store creating a fun, party atmosphere.

Luxottica Design + Construct Macquarie Park, Australia

PROJECT DESIGN TEAM
Timothy Bennett Luxottica Senior Designer
Michael Cramp Luxottica Design & Construction
  Manager

RETAIL DESIGN TEAM
Ben Mundy Luxottica Visual Merchandising Manager
Miah Sullivan Luxottica Marketing Director

CLIENT
Sunglass Hut, Sydney, Australia

GENERAL CONTRACTOR
Shopfitting Services Pty Ltd Kingston, QNS, Australia

OUTSIDE DESIGN CONSULTANTS
Moon Creative Surry Hills, NSW, Australia, *Graphics*

SUPPLIERS
Luxottica Australia Sydney, Australia, *Sunglasses*

PHOTOGRAPHER
Darren Leigh Roberts Photography Sydney, Australia

Colour with Asian Paints

New Delhi, India

SCOPE OF WORK According to the designers of Colour with Asian Paints, Indian customers are scared of color—at least when it comes to decorating. They find it a confusing and complicated category and they seek solutions that are easy and relevant to them. The goal of Asian Paints was to encourage customers to be more confident with color in their home décor projects. The company's ambition was to become the "ultimate décor and color experts," in India and in the region. The brand's promise is to remove the hassles and anxiety surrounding the selection of colors, and to offer a highly personalized color solution for each and every customer.

CUSTOMER JOURNEY There are three key themes that run throughout the Colour stores: 1) Colour Playground which incorporates Colour Cloud, Inspiration Dashboards and Colour 3D; 2) Collecting Inspirations which includes Colour Card, Be a Colour Star, Style Match and Colour Magazine; and 3) Customers evolving the store's content, creating a two-way dialogue between customer and brand. The Colour with Asian Paints store in Delhi is built on the notion of collaboration. The store delivers the retail equivalent of crowd sourcing: it openly invites customers to help tailor the store's

content. Through a series of feedback devices located throughout the store a dialog between customer and store develops — a concept unheard of in the category.

STORE PLANNING The use of Colour Cards are central to the in-store customer experience. As customers journey through the space they collect their inspirations on cards which utilize RFID technology. At the end of their journey, these inspirations are printed in a personalized Colour Magazine which can be taken home.

GOALS ACHIEVED As a result of the Colour with Asian Paint experience the Asian Paints brand has been fundamentally changed. They have become the decor and color experts in India, with a 35 percent increase in sales due to the many cans of paint sold in their adjacent dealer stores.

LIGHTING A dramatic lighting installation near the entrance is designed to engage customers emotionally as they enter the space and remove their anxiety surrounding the category. Inspired by Holi, the Indian festival of color, customers are invited to step on a color. Their decision alters the color of the cloud and of the entire store façade. The cloud uses RGB+W LEDs in 1000 custom aerated or frosted acrylic rods. The façade uses RGB+W LEDs set behind a custom Corian clad façade with routed discs of different depths. Both are connected to a central controller and motion sensors. RGB+W was used to ensure the color is rendered to the highest quality.

FIXTURING *Be a Colour Star* invites customers to experience how color can create a mood. A photo is taken of them with their favorite color mood and then shared via social media and placed on the cover of their personalized *Colour Magazine*. The designers' research indicated that customers in Delhi are very celebrity aware. As a result *Style Match* was created. The interactive digital game starring Bollywood megastar Saif Ali Khan matches customers to their perfect wall style based on a series of questions. Their resulting look is revealed on the adjacent wall.

Test your ideas with colour³ᴰ

VISUAL MERCHANDISING The space includes small roomsets in which the Inspiration Dashboards are located. Customers are invited to play with the dashboard and learn how color can transform a space and how light affects color. The results are demonstrated live in each room. On the back wall of the store (above) the full range of Asian Paints' colors is displayed on small painted cubes. Customers can choose their favorite color combinations and, guided by a Colour Consultant, can visualize their ideas in a virtual room on a nearby screen. The cubes can be spun to fine-tune the color sections—one way to darken and the other to lighten.

FITCH Singapore

PROJECT DESIGN TEAM
Darren Watson
Mariani Manja
Jessalynn Chen

CLIENT
Asian Paints Ltd.

GENERAL CONTRACTOR
NSA Delhi, India

OUTSIDE DESIGN CONSULTANTS
inProjects *Project Management*
Lighting Design Partnership *Lighting*
Experiential Design Lab *Digital Execution*

PHOTOGRAPHY
Jonny Lang and Mark Moreve from Real Spirit

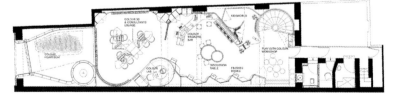

FIRST FLOOR PLAN
NOT TO SCALE

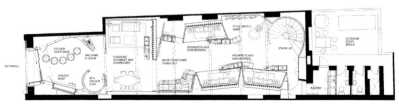

GROUND FLOOR PLAN
NOT TO SCALE

SantaCruz Pharmacy
Santa Cruz de Tenerife, Spain

SCOPE OF WORK MARKETING-JAZZ was tasked with an integrated design for a new brand concept in the Spanish pharmacy sector. The concept for SantaCruz Pharmacy is "A healthy world," and the 3,229 sq. ft. space is organized into categories to make self-service shopping easy and pleasant.

STORE PLANNING The pharmacy is divided into areas according to the products being sold, the desired shopping experience and the brand positioning. Special care has been taken to ensure that customer traffic flows and covers the whole pharmacy. The customer journey starts with the healthy sensations of beauty and natural products and displays, followed with medical product categories, ends with children's products and orthopedics. There are waiting areas for the elderly next to the counters, enabling them to be served without having to get out of their seats and with the pharmacy staff doing their "health shopping" for them. The design is meant to create specialized areas within the pharmacy for different categories and eliminate the traditional counters to avoid impersonal service and bring the pharmacists closer to the customer. The idea is for the pharmacist to accompany customers when making their "health purchase," and become a "personal shopper" for health products.

LIGHTING Every product is organized into categories and, to facilitate the identification of products, categories are clearly labeled. The furniture is illuminated using layers with a combination of white and yellow LED lighting to convey a sensation of warmth. The product and walls are illuminated using movable spotlights which provide extra impact thanks to a combination of halogens and halides. Also, natural lighting is provided by the glass wall.

FINISHES The materials were selected to give the impression of being in a "Future-Eco-Chic" pharmacy. Ceramic floors, furniture made from natural pine and white lacquered wood, crafted frame moldings, natural stones, plexiglass, and textile set up the ambiance and product presentation.

VISUAL MERCHANDISING Along one wall medications are presented on a large periodic table of the elements—providing a pleasant surprise to the shopper. The smile of discovery elicited is certainly unusual in the sector and makes for a memorable shopping experience. An area near the entrance offering cosmetics features a "make-up bar" where technology is used to provide customers with an analysis of their skin and the most suitable combination of cosmetic products. Throughout the space, crafted frame mouldings and natural stone reinforce the impression of the high quality, multi-brand products.

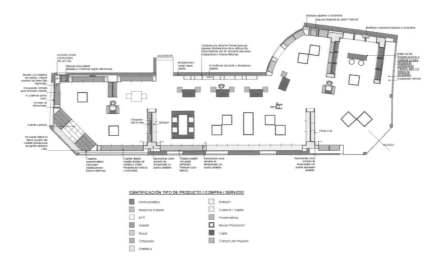

FIXTURING Fixtures have clean and minimal designs with straight lines. The use of different materials/colors are key to ease of shopping. All the materials where locally sourced from Santa Cruz de Tenerife island.

GOALS ACHIEVED The design has become a reference for pharmacies in the Spanish market and leads the way into the future of the pharmacy sector in the market. Even with many of today's consumers in a conservative spending mood, the new concept has seen a significant increase in sales and has attracted better employees.

MARKETING-JAZZ Madrid, Spain

PROJECT DESIGN TEAM
Carlos Sánchez de Pedro Aires Concept, Furniture Design, Visual
  Merchandising and Overall Creativity Supervision
Elena de Andrés Illustrations and Sketches.
Maria del Pilar Portela Planimetry
Natalia Aires Graphic Design

CLIENT
Mrs. Elsa Acosta, Santa Cruz de Tenerife, Spain

TECHNICAL ARCHITECT
Juan Antonio Santa Cruz de Tenerife, Spain

GENERAL CONTRACTOR
Llar proyectos arquitectura Santa Cruz de Tenerife, Spain, Juan Antonio

OUTSIDE DESIGN CONSULTANTS
Microlights Barcelona, Spain, *Lighting*

SUPPLIERS
Cofares Santa Cruz de Tenerife, Spain, *Carpentry*

PHOTOGRAPHER
Ikuo Maruyama Madrid, Spain

AT&T Michigan Avenue Flagship Store

North Michigan Ave., Chicago, IL

SCOPE OF WORK The project involved the strategic evolution of AT&T's retail experience into a one-of-a-kind store at the heart of Chicago's Magnificent Mile shopping district. The project is a complete renovation of a 10,000 sq. ft. single-level tenant space on the corner of N. Michigan and Ontario Streets. The scope included brand strategy and translation for retail, complete reinvention of the entire store experience, look and feel, including fixture design, merchandise strategies, integrated technologies, interactive experiences and sales process evolution.

BRAND PROMISE At the core of AT&T's mission is a commitment to deliver the future in a way that is relevant, approachable and friendly. AT&T's tagline, "Rethink Possible" is a call to action that is open and limitless; a perfect mix of optimism, energy and enthusiasm, grounded with a sense of warmth and approachability. The designers created a place where this promise can come to life, and where the line between technology and humanity is blurred.

CUSTOMER JOURNEY The overall layout was designed to be open, inviting and organized—creating a customer journey that is intuitive, fun and effortless. The journey presents five key moments where a customer can have immersive experiences and comfortable connections with staff. The Brand Entry is a point of decompression, with ambient brand elements. The Apps Bar allows customers to learn about the newest apps from "apps tenders." Lifestyle Boutiques are followed by the Gallery, where customers receive VIP-level service, and on the Experience Platform, 12 ft. high video panels bring product vignettes to life. Throughout the store the designers created a variety of places for face-to-face connections, to change the sales experience from "transaction to interac-

tion." Traditional cash wraps were eliminated and replaced with mobile landing stations, café-style learning tables, and sit-down lounge areas, all used by iPad armed staff.

FIXTURING & FINISHES A new family of fixtures was developed specifically for this store using a combination of wood, white solid surface and thick acrylic elements. The fixtures utilize flexible and modular acrylic pads for product storytelling and interactive experiences, and are organized to create a fun and communal shopping experience. It was important for the finishes to be inviting to shoppers while staying true to AT&T's technology presence. This was achieved through the warmth of reclaimed teak wood juxtaposed with crisp white modern fixtures and glass elements—all balanced with accents of AT&T's signature orange color.

SUSTAINABILITY The project was designed with sustainability and LEED Gold certification in mind. Highlights include an LED lighting package; use of reclaimed and regionally sourced, low-VOC materials and fixtures; and a focus on waste diversion and recycling of construction waste.

ENVIRONMENTAL GRAPHICS One of the unique aspects of the project is the integrated video technology that is interwoven throughout the entire design. The design utilizes over 150 LED monitors to create a rich and dynamic "brand canvas," used for both wayfinding and to set the stage for each experience area.

VISUAL MERCHANDISING The visual merchandising utilizes storytelling to present products in lifestyle collections. Experience vignettes include a mix of residential-styled fixtures, furniture, props and Chicago-themed elements. Most products are presented as "connected solutions" combining device, accessory and app into a single story. The design also creates spaces that allow for face-to-face customer and sales rep interactions, such as at the relaxed sit-down point-of-sale area in the "Gallery" space.

LIGHTING Key elements include trimless recessed spots for a clean, crisp look in the hard ceilings, adjustable spots in the open ceilings, and mirrored globe pendants to bring a sense of fashion to the experience. Linear fixtures in the floor and ceiling create a modern vibe on the Experience Platform.

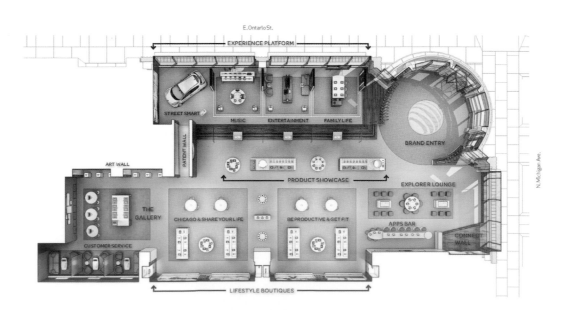

GOALS ACHIEVED This project moves away from traditional telecom retailing, showcasing how mobile devices are integrated into everyday life, not on the device itself. The store experience is designed to humanize technology, in a way that is fun, interactive and approachable. This comes to life in the "Lifestyle Boutiques" and the "Experience Platform" where products are presented in focused collections combining devices, apps, and accessories into rich and relevant stories.

Callison Seattle, WA

PROJECT AND RETAIL DESIGN TEAM
Callison Seattle Team
Alex Shapleigh Design Principal
Michelle McCormick Project Manager
Ryan Gorman Senior Designer
Feras Afani Ruzik Design
Mitch Pride Design
Glen Huntley Design
Jenn Cheung Brand Strategy
Scott Harris Architecture
Scott Homan Architecture
Callison Los Angeles Team
Tracy Woods
Amber Richane
Hee Jee Lee
AT&T Team
Mike Chisholm Retail Real Estate & Store Design
Lourdes Burson Retail Real Estate & Store Design
Bodie Adams Retail Real Estate & Store Design
Maria Simpson Marcom/Visual Merchandising
Shelley Setloff Marcom/Visual Merchandising
Mary Jenkins Digital Experiences
Christie Beals Digital Experiences
Pam Temple Customer Experience

Anne Marie Blandino Customer Experience
Gregg Heard Brand
Carl D. Ceresoli Technology
Tim Johnson Technology
Andrew McTighe Technology
Jeni Bell Product Marketing
Jeremy Duncan Product Marketing
Maureen Cardinallo Construction Management

CLIENT
AT&T, Atlanta, GA

ARCHITECT
Callison Seattle, WA

GENERAL CONTRACTOR
Healy Construction Crestwood, IL

OUTSIDE DESIGN CONSULTANTS
Razorfish Atlanta, GA, *Digital Experiences*
The Integer Group, Dallas, TX, *Visual Merchandising*
Sean O'Connor Lighting, Beverly Hills, CA, *Lighting Design*
Ædifica Case Engineering, St. Louis, MO, *Engineering*
Man Made Music New York, NY, *Sonic Branding*

SUPPLIERS
Midwest Store Fixtures University Park, IL, *Fixture Fabrication*
RCS Innovations Milwaukee, WI, *Fixture Fabrication*
Impact Displays Group, LLC Carlstadt, NJ, *Merchandising Displays*
D3LED Displays *LED Displays*
Tandus Flooring *Carpet*
Haworth Seattle, WA, *Raised Flooring*
Grainger Forest Park, GA, *Lighting*
Element Generation Brands *Lighting*
Lightolier Seattle, WA, *Lighting*
TerraMai White City, OR, *Reclaimed Teak*
Arper Inform Contract *Furniture*
Coalesse *Furniture*
KnollStudio Seattle, WA, *Furniture*
Priority Sign Sheboygan, WI, *Signage*

PHOTOGRAPHER
Chris Eden Seattle, WA

Groom Spa

Cheltenham, Victoria, Australia

GOALS ACHIEVED The new spa concept saw the number of treatments increase from 190 to 480 per week. The facade is aesthetically in contrast to its immediate context and as such draws interest and curiosity from the mall. This generates an invitation into the store, with materials, furniture and lighting combining to generate the notion of warmth, familiarity and comfort—indulgent yet accessible.

SCOPE OF WORK Located in a suburban shopping mall, Groom Spa is a day spa and retailer of high-end skin care products. The designers were tasked with the creation of a space that challenged the traditional notions of a day spa experience. The brief called for spaces for retailing with significant opportunities for visual merchandising, grooming (group treatments, manicures and pedicures), communal gathering and private treatments.

CUSTOMER JOURNEY The industrial steelwork, interspersed with lush greenery and delicately detailed timber signage, provides incentive to enter the spa. The elegant brass doorhandle is indicative of the luxury within. Inside, customers are transported from the mall setting into an immersive day spa experience. While each function within the store has its own identity, there are no formal boundaries separating them.

ENVIRONMENTAL GRAPHICS The traditional behind-the-counter service model has been eliminated with the creation of a fluid space with identifiable functional areas. Wayfinding is facilitated through visual connections and a large window provides a glimpse of other services that are offered beyond.

STORE PLANNING The space is divided into two areas: public zone and treatment room zone. The public zone houses the display and the manicure/pedicure areas. The dominating element here is the expansive wall of salvaged timber. The treatment room zone contains five treatment rooms.

FIXTURING & FINISHES A chamfered edge-ply box element sitting within the display wall at eye level ensures that products occupy prime display space. A palette of salvaged/recycled timber adds warmth to the space, against neutral warm greys and edge ply surfaces. The hints of polished brass add an old-worldly touch.

LIGHTING Lighting is critical for both functionality and mood within the spaces. The front-of-house zone has a subdued low level of light with bright patches of warmth for task lighting acting as a beacon to draw the eye into the depths of the store. The overall effect is atmospheric.

VISUAL MERCHANDISING The steel framed shelving system with plywood shelf inserts spans one entire side of the store. Interspersed with high-end French skin care products are salvaged books, coffee machine, curios and creeping plants.

SUSTAINABILITY Salvaged timbers from the previous tenant are used throughout on the walls and the flooring. The majority of furniture and display items are recycled and the devil's ivy creeper improves the air quality within the store.

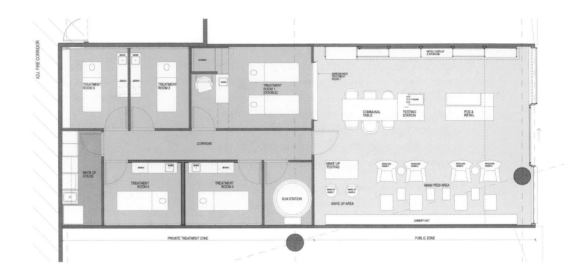

BRANDING The designers reinterpreted the day spa experience by presenting a space that reflected a lifestyle to which both male and female shoppers might aspire—but not be intimidated or alienated by. The store design was created with the intention of evoking the feeling of a space that is at once homey, familiar and comforting, rather than the perception of being in a space in which the sale of goods and services transpires. The designer also set out to create a space that would evolve with time, with plantings that would colonize the space and displays of books and curios that could be built upon.

BRAND PROMISE The client had a clear vision for a warm, inviting and original space, unlike the sterile, hard-edged spaces typical for this category. Complex functional requirements are interpreted as experiences that are memorable and distinct, providing a respite from the hustle and bustle of the bright, crowded and noisy mall experience.

Pinto Tuncer Pty Ltd Collingwood, Australia

RETAIL DESIGN AND ARCHITECT
Pinto Tuncer Pty Ltd Collingwood, Australia

OUTSIDE DESIGN CONSULTANTS
David Novak and Associates David Novak

CLIENT
Katherin Simpson

PHOTOGRAPHER
Greg Blakey, Lynton Crabb Melbourne, Australia

GENERAL CONTRACTOR
Crak Shopfitter Pty Ltd Allan Kansley

New Balance Boston
Boston, MA

BRAND PROMISE New Balance is all about performance. From the first arch supports to the latest performance technology, the brand's goal has always been helping people achieve their maximum potential and "Making Excellent Happen." New Balance Boston is both experiential and aspirational, helping consumers discover and reconnect with New Balance while championing the latest innovative products. The store honors Boston's role in New Balance's evolution as well as the legacy of local athletic heroes.

SCOPE OF WORK The brief called for a retail design for a 2,800 sq. ft. commercial property, including complete base building architectural, storefront design (landmarked), interior design, fixture design, lighting design and graphic design.

CUSTOMER JOURNEY New Balance Boston provides a window into the design and development process with an RFID technology wall and a live feed showcasing New Balance's domestic product manufacturing in Lawrence, MA. Projection mapping on the back transom windows plays a prominent role in communicating with consumers in a new and innovative way. Heard throughout the space is a custom athletic music profile that is upbeat and exciting. Product experts are on hand to complete the experience.

BRANDING New Balance Boston champions the company's history of "Making Excellent Happen" by taking the consumer through the company's rich heritage to the modern performance products of today. This journey is represented with the use of materials original to the building—approximately the same age as New Balance, 100-plus—layered with modern materials and textures including neon green track lines, digital projection mapping and glass statement walls.

ENVIRONMENTAL GRAPHICS The RFID technology wall has product technology tags that invite consumers to explore. Marathon bibs have been hand stamped into the plaster on the walls along with the map of the Boston marathon. A neon New Balance logo serves as a brand beacon within the store. Bold colorful graphics are layered with sleek panes of glass and antique 18th century hemlock. Neon track lines serve as colorful wayfinders. Images of current athletes live next to historical images, showcasing the journey in "Making Excellent Happen."

LIGHTING Large pendants were used to mimic the company's industrial manufacturing heritage, creating a low ambient light level. Suspended track heads with accent lights and wall washers highlight products and branding. In the windows, exposed cable-mounted lights are used to create sparkle and highlight product.

SUSTAINABILITY New Balance Boston demonstrates its commitment to sustainability through green design initiatives including utilization of original base building materials and 75% use of vintage/reclaimed materials and furniture in the fixture package.

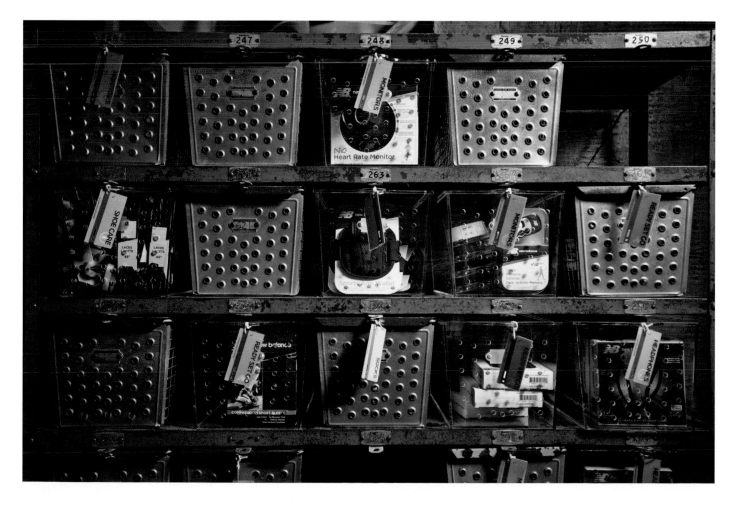

FIXTURING & FINISHES The fixture package was designed to bridge the rich history of the brand. Sleek metal perimeter systems are combined with vintage furniture and repurposed statement antiques on the floor. Mobile POS stations are made from a vintage tool cabinet that is split in two. Footwear, apparel and accessories are merchandised in vignettes, presenting product narratives alongside multi-layer graphic expressions. New Balance wanted every touchpoint of the experience to deliver on authenticity and character. They utilized reclaimed fire doors as the background for the statement RFID technology wall and reused the building's original fire door grilles (previously embedded in the wall), original brick, and original penny tile floor. Although damaged, the original tile floor was patched with new concrete to make a modern mosaic. On the perimeter the designers layered 18th century Hemlock wood with modern glass panes and metal outrigger poles.

GOALS ACHIEVED The designers honored the original architecture and design elements of the 100-year-old space while marrying the historical and cutting-edge performance messages. The resulting store pays homage to the "spirit of the runner" at the finish line of the Boston Marathon while also projecting an "underground" sneakerhead vibe.

New Balance Lawrence, MA

PROJECT AND RETAIL DESIGN TEAM
Bob Neville Director Global Creative, New Balance
Kirsten Marchand Senior Store Environments Manager, New Balance
Mark Keegan Creative Marketing Manager, New Balance

ARCHITECT
Perkins + Will Boston, MA

GENERAL CONTRACTOR
Structure Tone, Inc. Boston, MA

OUTSIDE DESIGN CONSULTANTS
ALU New York, NY, *Fixtures*
LX2 Hamden, CT, *Graphic Design*

IDL Worldwide East Butler, PA, *Graphic Design*
HLB Lighting New York, NY, *Lighting Design*
Nikole Nelson New York, NY, *Art*

SUPPLIERS
Klip Projection Philadelphia, PA, *Audio/Visual*
EarthCam Hackensack, NJ, *Audio/Visual*
Muzak/touch LLC Fort Mill, SC, *Music*
ALU New York, NY, *Fixtures*
2nd Story Wood Charlotte, NC, *Fixtures*
idX Columbia, MD, *Fitting Stools*
Nor'East Salvage South Hampton, NH, *Antique Wood*
Olde Good Things New York, NY, *Antiques*
RT Facts, Inc Kent, CT, *Antique Fire Doors*
Strawser and Smith Brooklyn, NY, *Furniture*

DWR Stamford, CT, *Chairs*
Clayton Gray Home Tampa, FL, *Furniture*
Baynes Electric Brockton, MA, *Lighting*
Barn Light Electric Titusville, FL, *Lighting*
Lifestyle & Trimco New York, NY, *Mannequins/Forms*
Van Stry Design Malden, MA, *Visual/POP*
Cahill Displays Boston, MA, *Visual/POP*
ICL Imaging Framingham, MA, *Signage/Graphics*
Benjamin Moore Paint Montvale, NJ, *Paint*
Poyant New Bedford, MA, *Exterior Signage*

PHOTOGRAPHER
Conor Doherty Boston, MA

engelbert strauss Workwear Store

Bergkirchen, Germany

SCOPE OF WORK The objective was to design a real workwear store for engelbert strauss that offers a broad variety of workwear and accessories all made by the company. The values and emotions of workwear had to appear in the store in a real and honest way while being easily understood by the client. It is the first workwear store of this size and meant to attract a broad group of customers. The goal of the new store design is to strengthen the brand and be a prototype for all upcoming stores.

GOALS ACHIEVED The new store defines workwear in a completely new way. Never before was buying clothes for work given these kind of emotions and looks. This is a real store for real craftsmen who need good quality workwear, yet the visual presentation is eye-catching, original and fun. The retail concept navigates customers through the store, in which all trades are represented by means of materials deriving from that trade's working environment. This results in a high level of competence and honesty.

CUSTOMER JOURNEY The huge, one-level, 27,986 sq. ft. space is given structure with emotional focus points, different segments and color themes. This is mainly done with space-defining elements instead of endless corridors that negatively appear like bowling alleys. Here customers always see a focus point or some kind of highlight element that emotionally guides them.

ENVIRONMENTAL GRAPHICS The store concept is built on design elements such as ceiling elements, focus areas, highlight zones (e.g. shoe area, wood island or bird's nest) and theme walls referring to the product and material world of the trades, thus evoking emotions. The wayfinding utilizes signs that are used in street work and other workwear surroundings.

LIGHTING Focused lighting is mixed with HIT floods and spots on suspended light tracks. A special cove lighting system intensifies the intended merchandise group categorization thus emphasizing the desired store structure and customer navigation. The ambient light level in the corridors is low to allow high levels of focused light on the walls and products. Decorative lighting elements refer to the product world (e.g. shovel luster) thus creating an emotional bond to the trades.

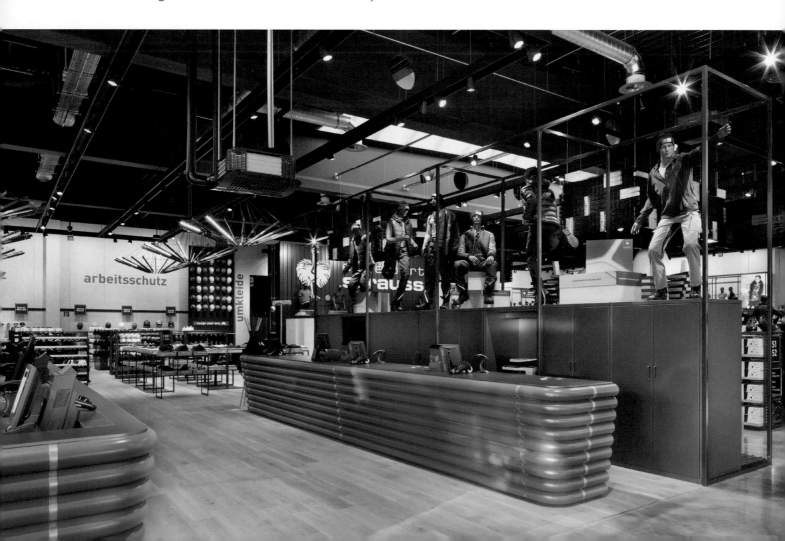

BRAND PROMISE The brand invites consumers to experience the world of workwear from a new and surprising perspective. In principle this is just what many lifestyle brands do: they use the looks and materials from the working-class world to make their products seem more "real." Here, however, the products are the real thing, the retailer is creating a true—and highly original—synthesis of product and lifestyle. The modern and professional merchandise of engelbert strauss workwear appeals to customers well beyond those employed in the working crafts. By presenting workwear products in a new context and using materials and elements from the working environment for the store design (e.g. shovels to create a luster or cable reels to replace display tables) the design shows courage and speaks the language the customer can truly identify with. Trust and competence are expressed via the use of honest materials such as rough wood and hot rolled metal and by the above mentioned references to the trades.

FIXTURING & FINISHES Merchandising fixtures are interpretations of tools and workmen's surroundings. All decorative product display elements derive from the working environment and are thus unusual and surprising in classic retail design—they always put a smile on the shopper's face. Rough wood, hot rolled metal, perforated brick walls, saws, drilling machines, cable reels, pallets, tension belts and various other allusions to the working environment not only play with the merchandise topic but above all stimulate customers' interests and evoke emotions.

VISUAL MERCHANDISING Visual merchandising extends the role of the store design and aims at transporting the customer into the real world of workwear. The merchandise is not presented as in a hardware store but much more like in a retail store.

plajer & franz studio gbr Berlin, Germany

PROJECT AND RETAIL DESIGN TEAM
Alexandra Theodoridis Project Manager
Stefanie Klug
Ute Häkel
Christopher Raabe

CLIENT
engelbert strauss GmbH & Co. KG Biebergemünd, Germany

ARCHITECT
plajer & franz studio gbr Berlin, Germany
IGV Projekt Consulting GmbH Fulda, Germany

GENERAL CONTRACTOR
engelbert strauss GmbH & Co. KG Biebergemünd, Germany

OUTSIDE DESIGN CONSULTANTS
Schleifenbaum Design & Project GmbH *Store Construction*
Ansorg GmbH *Lighting*

PHOTOGRAPHER
Ken Schluchtmann, diephotodesigner.de Berlin, Germany
Dirk Daehmlow

Hieber's Frische Center

Bad Krozingen

The food markets owned by the Hieber family have long been trendsetters in German food retailing. The store in Bad Krozingen is no exception. Its unusual architecture includes matte black paint and an exterior wall that inclines 15 degrees. The most innovative aspect of the design, however, is the creation of "merchandise worlds." Individual departments contrast in materials, floor coverings and lighting while maintaining a harmonious whole. Minimalist line drawings and black-and-white lettering on the walls identify each department, creating a signage system that runs through the entire market. "Buy and learn" is the motto. Instructional panels give product information and serve as design elements.

The Liverpool department store in Interlomas, a suburb of Mexico City, successfully combines the functions of a park and shopping center. In addition to being a department store, Liverpool becomes a public space and plays a new role as a social meeting place. The round, futuristic-looking building with a silver façade is now the flagship of the Liverpool chain. Its four floors, with a total of 30,000 square metres of retail space, are connected by an atrium that is flooded with daylight. Changing materials and colors create warmer shades as customers ascend. In this way they discover a whole new world on each floor and encounter impressive visual merchandising. The climax is the parklike rooftop garden covering 3,000 square meters, which includes a gourmet food area. (Liverpool Interlomas is also shown on page 30 of this book.)

Louis Vuitton Island Maison

Singapore

The Louis Vuitton Island Maison store occupies one of two glass pavilions on an island at Singapore's Marina Bay Sands resort. This is the first Maison store in southeast Asia. The asymmetrical steel and glass buildings were designed by architect Moshe Safdie and the interior, with a nautical theme, was designed by American architect Peter Marino. Elegant teak and chrome, plus sails that protect the façade from sunlight, emphasize the maritime style of the light-filled pavilion. From the centre customers have access to the various departments, including a bookstore, gallery, sun deck and — a first for the retailer — a "travel room." Visitors reach the Louis Vuitton Island via a walkway from the shore, via a tunnel from the Marina Bay Sands shopping mall, or on a special boat from the store's own jetty.

The transparent architecture of the Walnut Creek store—which makes it seem almost like a museum—offers a splendid view of the San Francisco region's East Bay. This panorama also inspired the interior design. Incident daylight connects the store with the surrounding landscape in a way achieved by few other stores. Bright, warm colors, glass and metal enhance the feeling of transparency and openness in the sales area. The store also features 163 works of art that are permanently integrated in the interior. The most conspicuous objects are two kinetic sculptures by local artist Ned Kahn that cover whole sections of the façade, with vertical fins moving in the wind.

El Palacio de Hierro Interlomas

Paseo Interlomas Mall, Interlomas, Mexico City, Mexico

The stunning new El Palacio de Hierro Interlomas epitomizes luxury retailing and asks of itself and its customers, "How may worlds fit into a palace?" The answer is as many worlds as you care to explore. Within a plan that eliminates linear corridors shoppers are offered an organic way to move about the space. "A direct communication is established with visitors through whimsical, sophisticated and functional spaces," states the design team.

El Palacio de Hierro (the Palace of Iron) recently opened its first new store in 13 years within Mexico City's Metropolitan Zone. The stunning new store in Interlomas epitomizes luxury retailing and asks of itself and its customers, "How may worlds fit into a palace?"

The answer is as many worlds as you care to explore. The three-floor, 27,000 square meter (more than 88,500 sq. ft.) sales floor showcases different areas—or worlds—within a plan that breaks away from conventional store planning and eliminates linear corridors. Consumers are instead offered a more natural way to move about the space and discover the merchandise. "A direct communication is established with visitors through whimsical, sophisticated and functional spaces," states the design team.

The project took two years as Fanny Schuller, El Palacio's Director of Visual Presentation and her team worked with national and international designers including PDT International to realize the unique space. "The result is a new generation store," explains the designers. "Today's customers are attracted to very different retail spaces such as small-concept boutiques and Palacio is conscious of this shift in client tastes. In this new store, we compete with these alternative distribution channels, but still express the same core brand values that we always have."

The El Palacio de Hierro stores are famous for their dramatic façades and this one is no exception. Renowned architect, Javier Sordo Madaleno was entrusted with the project and the resulting façade, an expression of contemporary luxury, is impossible to miss. Its triangular shape and 6,000 sq. meters of black granite have already made it an icon in the neighborhood.

Inside the store, the challenge was to create a natural flow between the three floors and the terrace and encourage customers to navigate the store with complete assurance. The solution is a circular design that surrounds a central atrium. The atrium serves as an access point to all the different "worlds" that Interlomas has to offer, while ensuring that shoppers can easily identify where they are, and where they want to go. Each world the customer enters has a different personality and evokes a different emotion.

"It's about creating an experience... changing the perception of the customers when they come into the store," sums up Schuller.

This is the first department store in Mexico to eliminate traditional point-of-sale print communication and turn entirely to digital signage. Custom screens, 115 in total, continuously project content created exclusively for the retailer and its partner brands. This content—the "Palacio Channel"— is unlike anything the customer would see on TV, or elsewhere, and ranges from lifestyle stories to product advertising. In addition to the 200 sq. meter screen (the largest in Latin America) on the façade and the huge screen in the atrium, each area within the store has its own signage to "speak" for it, involving the shopper at every turn.

Grupo Sordo Madaleno Mexico City
El Palacio de Hierro Team Mexico City
PDT International Fort Lauderdale, FL

ARCHITECT
Grupo Sordo Madaleno Mexico City

ARCHITECT/DESIGN
El Palacio de Hierro Team Mexico City

DESIGN
PDT International Fort Lauderdale, FL

DESIGN/STORE FIXTURES
Jorge Puente Visual Center Buenos Aires
Thinc, Mexico City

DIGITAL SIGNAGE
Content/Teran Mexico City

DIGITAL SIGNAGE/ENGINEERING
Sateliite Store Link (SSL) Mexico City

PROJECT MANAGEMENT
Grupo Rioboo Mexico City

STORE FIXTURES
ALU New York, NY
Elevations Inc. San Francisco, CA
Stor Mexico City

TECHNOLOGY
Sharp Corporation Mexico Mexico City
Technology Tecnosolutions Mexico City

PHOTOGRAPHY
HAH Photography, Mexico City

Zara

Via del Corso, Rome, Italy

Duccio Grassi transformed a 1886 neo-renaissance building into a soaring retail space for the trendy offerings of Zara. Says Grassi, "With my first on-site visit I was taken with the unexpected and exceptional quality of the architecture and the original intentions of the architect, who had created extraordinary interior volumes with immense windows that open towards the city. However, the former tenant had closed off the windows." Grassi sought to restore the building's geometry—compact yet light with large surfaces of iron and glass.

Grassi describes his, and his team's efforts: "Frequently when we design retail spaces we have to drastically change historical buildings from what they were originally designed to be and the 'violence' we are forced to use on these places can contain the seed of beauty, of contrast, of the unexpected. In the case of the Palazzo Bocconi, it was originally designed as a commercial space. The volumes are made to be seen as a unit—the sight crosses the whole space. The volumes—the architecture—takes you by the hand and you can't do anything but follow them. Certainly, today's commercial spaces have changed when compared to a century ago. Today there are needs for safety and climate control—the amount of traffic has increased enormously and merchandising is very different. To restore the light, the lightness and the transparency to the whole space, the size of the original floors was essential and the central patio cannot host icons as it is an icon itself. You cannot add anything —you can only remove what does not fit. Finally, the project must create the harmony between the requirements and the architecture—the soul of the building. This task was simplified for us by the passion and competence of our client.

"On the exterior we have restored the windows to their original majestic size and reopened those partially closed on the Via del Corso and the Via San Claudio. We have also created a filter which acts as an osmotic membrane and embraces all floors inside the cube/building. Inside each window there is a double metal sheet shaped like a draped curtain. The openings of the two sheets are coincident: facing them you can see the outside—the sun, the rain, the city life. Passing by them you perceive light with different effects at different times of the day. Seen from inside the store the metal sheet is naturally fit for hanging of product or shelves for stacking.

"Working with the Ministry of Cultural Heritage, we repositioned the vertical connections—the public staircases as well as the safety stairways—and still maintained the integrity of the volumes. The modern false ceilings were eliminated and restored with Stucci (stucco). Travertine, the archetype stone of Rome, was used for the new flooring and the basement, which was originally closed to the public, now with all walls and false ceilings removed shows a forest of naked columns which reminds one of the Roman Basilica cistern in Istanbul.

The design of the fixtures is fresh and contemporary and creates a strong, modern identity for the space. The neutral color palette of the glass wall varies from white to dark gray as one moves up to the top floor—enabling the shopper to identify each floor by its color.

In the basement is the children's department. Women's wear is presented on the central floors while on the upper levels are men's wear.

Duccio Grassi Architects Italy

DESIGN TEAM
Duccio Grassi, Leader
Marco Porpora
Pich Tripasai
Nicola Fanesi
Claudia Cavina
Silvia Sirocchi
Maurizio Putignano
Mattia Villa

PHOTOGRAPHY
Andrea Martiradonna

Marimekko
Flatiron District, New York, NY

Sixty years ago Marimekko burst upon the decorating scene with bold colors, splashy designs and a light, effervescent spirit. There was a time when the sprightly patterns and stinging colors were "all the thing." Marimekko is back and it is back with its color and pattern as fresh as ever.

The Flatiron district of New York is abloom—again. With Eataly and many other top brand stores filling the streets it is "in" again. We quote from the Marimekko press release. "The new flagship store plays an important role in the building of Marimekko's profile and strengthening the brand image in the United States. The store has been built as an experience-rich meeting place in which Marimekko's varied colors and design idiom lead the customer from one inspiring mood to the next. The range embraces all product lines, and it is intended for the store to act as a showcase for new products in particular. The New York City store is based on the same concept as the flagship opened in Helsinki early this year."

With a mix of clothing, accessories, home fashion elements and fabric-by-the-yard, there is lots to see and lots to pick from. The designers took full advantage of the ceiling height by creating a natural wood cubicled fixture/partition for decorative pillows and metal racks for the rolls of fabric that to go up, up, up. Natural honey-toned wood appears throughout to complement the crisp whiteness of the envelope. Shelved and cubicled partitions divide the space into a series of workable and identifiable "shops." While perusing the selection of black, red and white garments suspended from the ceiling, customers can find bags and other "go-with" accessories in what are basically shop-within-shops created by the white semi-dividing walls.

The president and CEO of Marimekko, Mika Ihamuotila, said, "The store is the spearhead of our strategy for the United States and its mission is to showcase the whole world of Marimekko at its best and its full scope for American customers."

DESIGN
IMA, Japan and the Marimekko Design Team

PHOTOGRAPHY
Courtesy of Marimekko

The high-ceilinged space is all white—floors, walls, ceiling as well as the myriad pipes and ducts exposed overhead. However, the numerous squares of boldly patterned fabrics suspended from overhead along with the black-and-white fabric-covered rectangles that serve as lamp shades for pendant lamps within the cubes all tend to bring the more than 20 ft. ceilings down to a more human-size environment. The flashes and splashes of color and pattern overhead attract and delight but does not detract from what is shown on the sales floor.

A'maree's
Newport, CA

For the past 40 years, A'maree's has been an international fashion powerhouse operated by a fashion-forward family. Operated today by Dawn Klohs, Denise Schafer and Apryl Schafer, the daughters of the shop's founder Nancy Brown, the boutique sells the wares of fashion luminaries such as Balenciaga, Azzedine Alaia, Celine, Dries Van Noten, Lanvin, Sacai and others.

The new and expanded home for A'maree's flagship store is an historic 1960s modernist harbor-side structure with a distinctive scallop-edge roofline, soaring arched windows and 18.5 ft. ceilings. The building is located in Newport Beach and was originally designed by Ladd and Kelsey Architects of Pasadena, also designers of the Norton Simon Museum. In one of its incarnations the building served as a restaurant and all traces of that restaurant and its furnishings had to be removed and the building restored, as much as possible, to its original design to make room for A'maree's. Paul Davis Architects (PDA) of Los Angeles was charged with recreating this 8,100 sq. ft. palazzo of fashion, and filling the open space with all the amenities expected, and more, of a high fashion boutique.

Under the leadership of Paul Davis, the designers meticulously restored the structure to its original design intent. "Themes of transparency, reflectivity, layering and memory infuse the project through planning, architecture and materials. The atmosphere combines an almost domestic casual elegance with high end style," explains the design team. The entire shop is open and clients are invited to enjoy the view from the deck, where tea is served, and wander to the back-of-the-house where the dressing rooms and the kitchen are located.

From the outside and throughout the interior it is white-on-white—even to the polished concrete floors in the sales area. Two ornate brass chandeliers at the entry, also painted white, "contribute to a bright, spare environment, where salespeople, shoppers and merchandise bring artful warmth and color to the space." What was previously the dining room of the now-gone restaurant is the main retail floor. The tall ceilings soar over the floor and the original cruciform cast-in-place concrete columns that support the vaulted domes are now visible and chaste. Depressions left in the floor where the restaurant booths were removed are now filled with seashells "to create repeating circular ripples that extend the curved motifs throughout the building and interior." The semi-circular white plaster cash counter was created in the shape and structure of the now demolished exhibition kitchen.

"With its mix of industrial and elegance rooted in a remarkable synthesis of classic modernity and vaulted forms recalling an old world bazaar, the new A'maree's store has delighted old and new customers alike." It is "a palace of playful indulgence and sophisticated delights," while also "comfortable and casual reflecting Newport's lifestyle."

"With its mix of industrial and elegance rooted in a remarkable synthesis of classic modernity and vaulted forms recalling an old world bazaar, the new A'maree's store has delighted old and new customers alike." It is "a palace of playful indulgence and sophisticated delights," while also "comfortable and casual reflecting Newport's lifestyle."

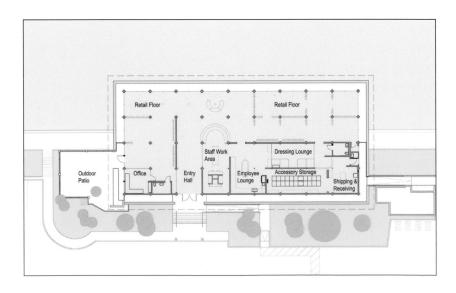

What was previously the dining room of the now-gone restaurant is the main retail floor. The tall ceilings soar over the floor and the original cruciform cast-in-place concrete columns that support the vaulted domes are now visible. The semi-circular white cash counter was created in the shape and structure of the now demolished exhibition kitchen.

Where the kitchen was once located is now the back-of-the-house area—behind the cash counter. "The design intent was to create a charged juxtaposition between the elegant white plastered public areas and the 'archaeologically exposed' back-of-house, now featuring a rich, warm palette of exposed rough concrete structure, original copper roof drain lines, all illuminated with shafts of sunlight through new skylights in the domed ceiling." Back here are the dressing rooms.

Paul Davis Architects (PDA) Los Angeles, CA

DESIGN TEAM
Paul Davis, AIA Principal in Charge
Gabriel Leung Project Designer
Sarah Knize
Ken Vermillion
Jennifer Williams

GENERAL CONTRACTOR
Summit General Contractors

LIGHTING
**Kaplan, Gehring, McCarroll Architectural
  Lighting / Conor Sampson Design**

MEP ENGINEER
RPM Engineers, Inc.

PHOTOGRAPHY
John Ellis, Paul Davis Architects

Scabal
Brussels, Belgium

The design directive given to the designers was to "tailor the perfect spatial concept, wedding the sophisticated fabric manufacturer to a British gentlemen's club atmosphere." The impression starts at the entrance where leather-covered frames line the walls and accessories, shirts, suits and shoes are displayed like artistic still-lifes. White, backlit ceiling panels—set in varying heights—complement the light limestone flooring, and deep-set light cubes in the ceiling correspond with the leather covered platforms used for additional presentation surfaces.

Scabal suits and fabrics are the very epitome of the British gentleman's style, with a shot of Hollywood glamour. Scabal suits are worn by personalities such as Barak Obama, Michael Douglas and even James Bond a.k.a. Daniel Craig. In creating the Scabal flagship store in Brussels, the designers at Blocher Blocher Partners had to "tailor the perfect spatial concept, wedding the sophisticated fabric manufacturer to a British gentlemen's club atmosphere."

The impression starts at the entrance to the almost 2,000 sq. ft. space where leather-covered frames line the walls and the merchandise is displayed like artistic still-lifes and dressed mannequins serve to introduce the fashions for which Scabal is noted. Also at the entrance is a stylized loom that introduces the Scabal logo: Scabal blue threads on two layers interwoven with the golden crowned lion symbol, emblazoned with the boldly curved "S."

The designers explain, "The space itself: an ode to exclusive couture; one might call it the deluxe version of a tailor's workshop. The customer passes through four zones: reception room, the treasure chamber, the inner courtyard and salon. All are done in tones of brown and gray; a perfect backdrop for displaying high quality fabrics." Following the entrance, the "treasure chamber," with its incisively grained walnut veneer panels set crosswise from floor to ceiling, is done "in a classical masculine style."

The design elements introduced in the entrance reappear in the "inner courtyard"—leather frames and cubes, limestone flooring, concrete walls and gray ceiling. This area leads seamlessly into the "salon" which embodies the British sophisticated spirit that is part of Scabal's fabrics. Here, fabric covered arm chairs are clustered around a leather covered Chesterfield-style table.

Scabal is now recognized throughout Europe as well as in the US, Japan and East Asia. The launching of this redesign of the Scabal shop is in answer to competition. Gregor Thissen, Scabal's CEO, says, "We are ready for the increased demand, ready for the targeted growth plans and ready for the competition." As the designers add, "We created a world that blends heritage with new beginnings; celebrated style as a platform for the more than 5,000 fabrics the firm produces. It's a place for today's cosmopolitan man and a tribute to the value of the label: perfect fabrics and timeless elegance."

The "treasure chamber," with its incisively grained walnut veneer panels set crosswise from floor to ceiling, is done "in a classical masculine style." Bales of cloth interspersed with books, collars and cuffs appear in the inset wooden wall cubes. "The display of the exclusive Suit #12 is a masterpiece of tailoring, lives up to the term 'treasure room'." A custom made cutting table, especially designed for this space, appears in the center of this room. The dressing/ fitting room where the tailor takes measurements and checks for a perfect fit. It is paneled in a fine walnut veneer.

The understatement of the interior courtyard is interrupted by a bold architectural element: a light-flooded patio that breaks into the room in the form of a glass cube. Framed by ivy, it forms a green oasis for a refreshing pause. Beyond is the "salon" where fabric covered arm chairs are clustered around a leather covered Chesterfield-style table—all resting on an anthracite colored carpet. A floor-to-ceiling bookshelf is filled with antique objects that relate to the tailoring trade and a Victorian era mirror is set over a sunken fireplace.

Blocher Blocher Partners Stuttgart, Germany

SHOP FITTING & GENERAL CONTRACTOR
Ganter Interior, Tauberbischofsheim, Germany

LIGHTING
elan Beleuchtungs & Elektroanlagen, Cologne, Germany

PHOTOGRAPHY
Nikolaus Koliusis, Stuttgart, Germany

Bing Harris & Co.

Albany, Auckland, New Zealand

The company's beginnings in "vast, timber-rafted warehouses" was the inspiration for the design of the new shop created by Pennant & Triumph. Taking their cues from the original warehouse structure from more than a century and a half ago, the designers used materials that were "natural, raw, authentic, and masculine—such as brick, steel, and woods. These elements have been taken and modernized for today's style-savvy customer." A pair of brick pilasters frame the entrance to the shop and a series of brick arches continues across the façade suggesting an old warehouse structure. The deep gray, almost black, matte finish of the brick serves as a sharp contrast for the messages inscribed on some of the façade spaces. The steel door is raw metal and carries the store name/logo.

If you are looking for heritage or tradition—and if you are from Australia or New Zealand—then the place to go for men's casual wear is Bing Harris & Co. Originally established in 1858 as general merchants and warehousemen, they started manufacturing dry goods, clothing and even footwear to become noted and respected suppliers of quality merchandise. Bing Harris & Co. clothing fuses "high level craftsmanship with affordable street-level style" and nothing makes them happier than knowing their customers love and enjoy wearing their clothes. "We invest in the product which is inspired from the sartorial style setters around the world."

Today the company still takes pride in their beginnings from "vast, timber-rafted warehouses." That concept was the inspiration for the design by the architectural firm of Pennant & Triumph for the retail space in Auckland. Taking their cues from the original warehouse structure from more than a century and a half ago, the designers used materials that were "natural, raw, authentic, and masculine—such as brick, steel, and woods. These elements have been taken and modernized for today's style-savvy customer."

The entrance to the shop is framed by a pair of brick pilasters and a series of brick arches continues across the façade suggesting an old warehouse structure. Proudly and recurring is the "est. 1858" notation underscoring the age and heritage of the firm. The shop interior is mostly white and gray. According to the designers, the brick wall that dominates a wide expanse behind the very long cash/wrap desk has a modern wash of matte white paint and strongly stated is—once again—the company logo hand painted with a distressed finish. On other key walls there are various old brand announcements that have been hand painted in a similar manner.

Wood plays an integral part in the design of the store and is used to further underscore the warehouse origin of the company. Plywood such as is used for shipping crates appears throughout while high, gloss finished raw wood packing pallets serve as elevations for mannequins as well as product display. All have the company logo sprayed on to further carry through the crate idea.

The space is interrupted by steel- and brick-faced columns. Red accents appear on the racking system, shelving and across the cash/wrap desk.

The white abstract mannequins appear in the open backed windows that flank the store entrance as well as on the floor and even atop some of the lower storage units. The dropped light tracks provide sparkle and highlights to the wall displays as well as the products arranged on the mid-floor fixtures. According to Pennant & Triumph, "The past is the basis for the design but the future is reflected in the treatment of these older elements."

Red accents appear on the racking system and on the shelving. In addition to the open-backed windows at the entrance, white mannequins appear on the floor and even atop some of the storage units. The dropped light tracks provide sparkle to the wall displays as well as the products arranged on the mid-floor fixtures.

The brick wall that dominates a wide expanse behind the very long cash/wrap desk has a modern wash of matte white paint and the company logo hand painted with a distressed finish. On other key walls there are various old brand announcements that have been hand painted in a similar manner.

Pennant & Triumph Auckland, New Zealand

DESIGN TEAM
Justin Rodriguez
Nik Rush

PHOTOGRAPHY
Kallum Mc Cloud

White Lounge

Wallisellen, Switzerland

Wallisellen is a suburb of Zurich, yet many brides-to-be are drawn to the cool, sleek white-on-white environment created by the Zoro family working with Lorenzo Sager that is the White Lounge. The sisters, Katia and Milena Zoro, who inherited the "bridal fashion gene" from their family, say "Wedding dresses and the wedding lifestyle have always been our passion" and that passion has been realized in a space of about 4,250 sq. ft. in the Designer Center in Wallisellen. Here the sisters have "lovingly created a paradise for romantic brides—and have turned it into a dream in white." The shop features a wide selection of bridal gowns of good quality and at moderate prices by international designers.

Billowing bridal gowns float through the almost totally white ambiance. Floors, walls and ceiling are white, the furniture and fix-

tures are white, and the gowns are white. To make the gowns stand out and apart from their surroundings the featured dresses are shown on headless black dress forms. The open-plan of the floor has been subtly divided into four gracious and generously proportioned individual consultation areas where family and friends can be comfortably seated to view the bride-to-be in her selections and voice their opinions. Soft draperies can be pulled across each space to provide privacy. In addition to a screened off presentation area, each has a changing area for the future bride as well as a special vitrine for bridal accessories.

The Umdasch Shopfitters of Switzerland provided the high gloss white with chrome accented furnishings used throughout.

The Zoro Family, Lorenzo Sager Wallisellen, Switzerland

SHOPFITTING
Umdasch Shopfitting, Switzerland

PHOTOGRAPHY
Courtesy of Umdasch Shopfitting

Piccino
City of Science, Valencia, Spain

The designer used fun and sunny colors and a pair of youngster icons based on the owner's children to enliven the white, nook-free space. Instead of using pieces with actual details, Ms. Palacios combined modular shelves with storage drawers with overlays of artworked vinyls for interesting details that were "dust-free." Humor becomes the element that glues it all together and keeps the shoppers, young and not-so-young entertained.

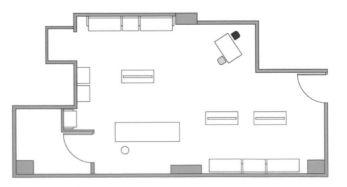

How does one design a shop for fine Italian imported clothes on a limited budget, in a space of only about 400 sq. ft., and keep it dust free because of the owner's allergies? How do you create enough space to show and store garments for children from 0 to 14 years of age? How do you do all the basic things and make the store inviting and attractive to parent and child alike? Those were only some of the problems facing Ana Milena Hernandez Palacio of the Masquespacio design studio of Valencia in Spain.

Using fun and sunny Crayola colors and a pair of youngster icons based on the owner's children, the designer found her inspiration. Instead of using actual pieces, Ms. Palacios combined modular shelves with storage drawers and overlays of artworked vinyls for details that were "dust-free." Humor became the element that glued it all together.

To keep the shop from getting cluttered, the designer used a modular shelf system that allows elements to be moved around easily. Each shelf contains a storage area and all the floor fixtures are on wheels, allowing for change. Depending upon season, or the arrival of new items, some areas might need to be compressed to allow another to expand. "In that way the space is best used without overwhelming the shopper with what could be 1000 pieces." There is even a kid's corner where children can play or be entertained.

Ms. Palacios sums it up, "From the beginning we knew it was impossible to use some objects for decoration due to our client's allergy but the biggest challenge without a doubt was the very low budget. Creativity is a powerful tool. When the budget is really low it may be more difficult to apply that creativity, but fortunately there are things such as stickers (vinyl paste-ups) we can use. Leaving a client happy and satisfied after finishing a project is the thing that makes me proud. It is important to be creative without losing the commercial requirements. Actually, when shoppers enter this store it is impossible for them to be indifferent to the environment. It causes an emotional response that favors the business"

The space is white and jumping with color and sprightly graphics accented with a fun attitude. The store's in-store characters also appear on posters and on the website.

Masquespacio Valencia, Spain

DESIGNER & GRAPHICS
Ana Milena Hernandez Palacios

PHOTOGRAPHERS
Inquietud & David Rodriguez of Cualiti

Kabiri

The Market, The Piazza, Covent Garden, London

The designers kept the focus on the product display by maintaining a dark monochromatic palette throughout. All the finishes on the walls, displays cases, upholstered panels and floor tiles are matte gray—apart from the York stone slabs on the basement floor. Reached by an open staircase with clear plastic sides, the basement presents an array of fine jewelry as well as a consulting room.

Located in Covent Garden in London, where once Eliza Doolittle of My Fair Lady fame sold her wilted flowers is The Market in The Piazza. Amid the structural and architectural remains of the old flower and produce market, savvy and fashion-forward shops are now tucked into the small spaces. One of them is Kabiri. As designed by Found Associates, of London, "The new store is an elegant and inviting space for customers to explore the rich variety of work available at Kabiri by 85 independent jewelry designers."

The presentation begins in the large display windows that face the covered walkways of Covent Garden's Market Hall. The display fixtures and cases that are set near the windows function as an attraction from the outside and for selling purposes inside the shop. Inside, the product offer is displayed on two levels in the 1,200 sq. ft. space with costume and fashion jewelry at ground level and an extensive array of fine jewelry presented in the basement level. In order for each jewelry designer to get as much display space as possible, each designer's work is displayed on an individual upholstered mat which has additional half and quarter sized mats placed on top to affect dynamic tiered displays for the collection. In addition there is a consulting and a changing room on the lower level which is reached by the open staircase with its clear plastic sides. The Kabiri logo runs between the floors "to encourage customers to explore the jewelry on both levels."

The new, beautifully-lit shop fulfilled all that Kabiri hoped for and makes available "the very best in contemporary jewelry design regardless of genre or price"—in a dramatic and dynamic setting where the space has been made to serve and enhance the product presentation.

PHOTOGRAPHY
Guy Archard

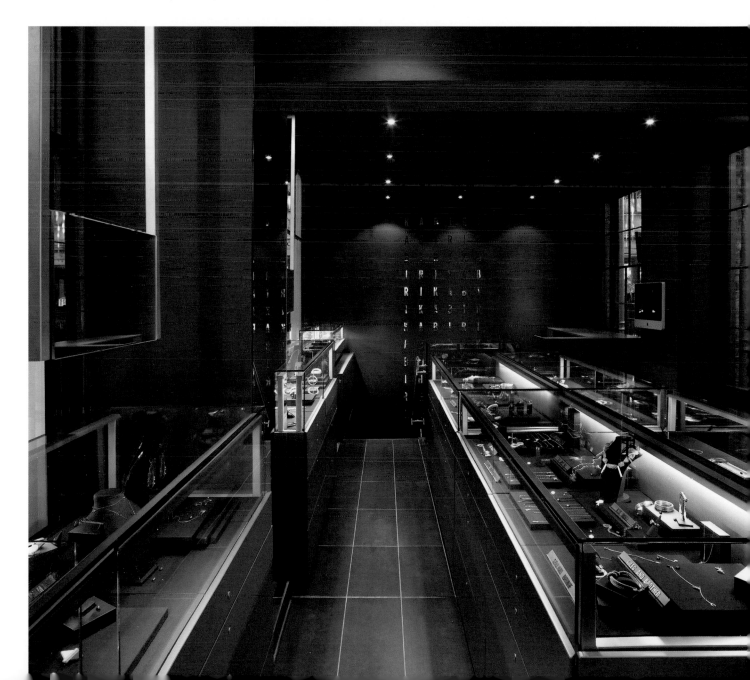

SKINS 6|2

Cosmopolitan Hotel, Las Vegas, NV

According to the designer, "SKINS 6|2 was inspired by the dynamic and ever-changing nature of street markets and refines the notion of freshly delivered crates of produce to stimulate shopper curiosity. Loose groupings, stacks of boxes and familiar fixturing keep the shop accessible and exciting. Generating this flexibility within the store was key in making the environment diverse, fresh, and accommodating for new products and services."

For their first store in the United States, the Dutch cosmetics retailer, SKINS 6l2, invited their "local talent"—the Uxus design firm of Amsterdam—to design the shop which is located in the new Cosmopolitan Hotel on the famous Strip in Las Vegas. With neighbors such as London's All Saints fashion shop and New York City's famous Blue Ribbon Sushi, it called for a design that would be noteworthy for the clientele—"the multicultural, city-chic, urban-minded and design-driven crowd."

Oliver Michell, a partner in Uxus, recognized that the location was the ideal platform for launching the brand and the concept. The challenge was "to create an inspiring venue to showcase some very exciting cosmetic and perfume brands, and inject some magic into the new-built space—keeping in mind the Vegas Factor."

The metal-covered, oversized and pattern-filled doors that dominate the façade of SKINS 6l2 more than suggest what will be going on inside the shop. Even before entering, the shopper can see, through the wide glass windows, the floating, metallic ceiling panel—hovering over the central space. It, like the doors, is filled

with repouseé patterns—designs hammered into the metal causing relief designs on the face. This ribbon of weathered, pressed tin ceiling tiles helps to create "a dramatic entrance and infuses the space with a deconstructed 'boudoir' attitude." The balance of the ceiling is blacked out and, in the rear of the shop, hang myriad circular translucent lamp shades. The neutrality of the setting—white, gray, black, light-colored wood and silvery metallics—allows the product packaging and display to step forward under the rows of spots that illuminate the wall shelf units and standing fixtures.

Dozens upon dozens upon dozens of assorted sizes and shapes of mirrors create a fascinating rear wall for the shop—the count actually more than one hundred. Ornate or simple, round, oval rectangular—tiny or large—filling the wall with sparkle and shimmer—they set the scene for the make-up consultancy area under that battery of lamp shades. The all-white furniture and the white wall behind the mirrors is contrasted by the black shelving fixture off to one side.

Most of the perimeter wall shelving consists of what looks like assorted rectangles of different sizes stacked helter-skelter atop one another creating a wall of interesting patterns—some boxes stepping forward—others recessed. Here you can see how Uxus has interpreted the "freshly delivered crates" that Michell noted. Here too we see the mixture of the white finish with the subtle light woods used on some of the "boxes." This free-form conglomeration is balanced by the simple open floor fixtures and some straightforward table displayers/fixtures.

"The overall store concept gives a sense of spontaneity and encourages shoppers to browse and discover their favorite products."

UXUS Amsterdam, The Netherlands

PARTNER
Oliver Michell

ARCHITECT
KGA Architecture

CLIENT
Supergaaf LLC

PHOTOGRAPHY
Courtesy of UXUS

Richard Chai Pop-up Shop

Under the High Line, West 23rd St., New York, NY

The designers at Snarkitecture, working closely with Richard Chai, carved from the confines of an existing structure underneath the High Line a glacial cavern in which Chai's garments were viewed. The High Line has become a gathering spot for locals and visitors alike. Deserted elevated train tracks that skimmed the western edge of Manhattan have been turned into a mile or more of walkway—a thing of beauty with flowers, foliage and a fabulous view of the Hudson River and New Jersey.

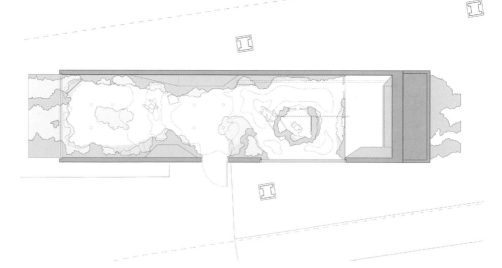

Pop up shops are popping up all over the place and sometimes in the least expected places. It is rare that a day or two goes by without another tiny shop popping onto the retail scene and then vanishing. Only in rare cases do they leave behind photos of what small, but effective wonders, they were. Fortunately, some designers do record their fly-into-the-night installations. And so, we bring you this creative pop-ups by a Brooklyn-based architecture firm called Snarkitecture founded by Alex Mustonen and Daniel Arsham.

It would help to appreciate their designs if we know something about the designers. They "operate between art and architecture." Their practice "focuses on the investigation of structure, material and program and how these elements can be manipulated to some new and imaginative purposes." The architect/artists are "searching for sites within architecture with the possibility for confusion and misuse. And make architecture perform the unexpected." And the unexpected is what we get in the installation shown here.

Richard Chai was honored in 2010 by the Council of Fashion Designers of America by being named as "Designer of the Year for Menswear." As part of the Building Fashion series presented by Boffo, the designers at Snarkitecture, working closely with Richard Chai, carved from the confines of an existing structure underneath the High Line this glacial cavern in which Chai's garments were viewed. (For those unfamiliar with the "High Line," it is a recent highlight for locals and visitors in NYC. Deserted elevated train tracks that skimmed the western edge of Manhattan have been turned into a mile or more of walkway—a thing of beauty with flowers, foliage and a fabulous view of the Hudson River and New Jersey).

Using a single material—white architectural foam—the creative designer cut the material by hand "to produce erosions and extensions of the sculpted walls and ceiling to create a varied landscape for the display of the Richard Chai Collection. The range of shelves, niches, hang bars and other moments embedded within the foam encourage the designer's [Chai's] eye for display." The result, as seen in these images, is a frozen place full of varied shapes and forms and serves as an art installation as well as a unique setting for merchandise.

When the Pop Up popped and was over, the material was returned to the manufacturer to be recycled into rigid foam insulation, and so—in a way—the exhibit lives on.

Using a single material—white architectural foam—the creative designer cut the material by hand "to produce erosions and extensions of the sculpted walls and ceiling to create a varied landscape for the display of the Richard Chai Collection." Shelves, niches and hang bars are embedded within the foam. The result is a frozen place full of varied shapes and forms and serves as an art installation as well as a unique setting for the merchandise.

Snarkitecture Brooklyn, NY

DESIGN
Alex Mustonen
Daniel Arsham

PHOTOGRAPHY
David B. Smith, Lexie Moreland

Timberland Pop-up Shop

Flatiron District, New York, NY

Timberland recently promoted its Earthkeepers™ programs and products from a kiosk installed for only four days in New York City's popular and trendy Flatiron district. In a novel approach to the pop-up shop, no products were actually sold from the tiny enclosure; instead emphasis was placed on educating the consumer and inviting participation in the company's various earth-friendly initiatives.

The kiosk itself was a model of eco responsibility. The circular body was constructed of recyclable trash—smashed plastic bottles and containers, 450 pounds in all, enclosed in recycled steel mesh. The eco-friendly materials list continued with reclaimed barn wood floors, FSC certified non-formaldehyde wood frames, low VOC latex paints, low energy lights, and Energy Star rated electronics. In short, every element of the kiosk was consistent with Timberland's message of ethical stewardship of the planet.

Timberland's line of Earthkeepers products were on display — both from windows inset in the mesh frame and on shelves inside the kiosk—and representatives were on hand to direct consumers to nearby retailers. Given equal emphasis in the kiosk were displays explaining the company's philosophy, methods and goals,

including information about organic cotton, P.E.T. plastic, and the Green Rubber™ used in Earthkeepers' boots.

Consumers could also browse an old-fashioned bulletin board fastened with information on Timberland's various local eco-minded partners, including the Million Trees NYC project, or browse a new-fashioned computer and participate by interactively planting a tree.

In a twist of fate, the kiosk was in place for an unusually early NYC snow storm—weather that surely reminded consumers of the importance of a sturdy pair of boots. Cassie Heppner, the Senior Manager of Field Marketing, reported, "We estimated a couple hundred visitors over the course of the four days. Due to the inclement weather Saturday we closed the booth early; however, consumers loved the booth. People commented that it looked like an art installation, but when they found out we were highlighting our Earthkeepers product it made perfect sense. Even the materiality of the booth supported our Earthkeepers message — create product with the environment in mind."

Camper Shoes

Soho, New York, NY

The single-story structure is located at the base of a 1975 trompe l'oeil mural by Richard Haas and is open to the ultra trendy Prince and Greene Streets in New York's Soho. Atop the flat roof is a triangular Paper Tube Structure that is a signature Shigeru Ban touch.

When a leading international shoe designer and retailer hires an internationally acclaimed architect to design their flagship store in one of New York City's top fashion areas it is something to take note of. The new Camper Store that opened on the corner of Prince and Greene Streets in Soho was designed by Shigeru Ban who is known for his "poetic" architectural style. As a spokesperson for Camper says, "The store is minimal, while at the same time playful. The store reflects innovative design consistent to Mr. Ban's work and incorporates his flare for ingenuity with beautiful modern design that remains the hallmark throughout all his projects."

The building is located in an historic district therefore required landmark approval. It also sits under a famous 1975 trompe l'oeil mural by Richard Haas. The building was completely gutted and transformed into the Camper retail outlet with 1,200 sq. ft. on both the ground and basement levels. Atop the flat roof is a triangular Paper Tube Structure that is a signature Shigeru Ban touch.

The existing bulkheads under each window were removed and replaced with sliding doors—making it possible to enter the store from various places. "When the doors are slid open the building becomes completely connected to the street, enlivening the street and acting like a covered bazaar." The effect is similar to the out-door bazaar only a few blocks away at Spring and Wooster Streets.

A bold red wall with white letters spelling out the Camper name is the first sight one gets of the store. The designers explain, "It isn't until one enters the store that one sees a disintegration of the letters and discover the shoe display revealed in cubbies arranged in a 45 degree angle in plan behind the red wall. The 45 degree angle is echoed in a polished concrete floor with epoxy red stripes and a corrugated metal ceiling that is red on one side and white on the other. At the far end of the space is a mirror that simultaneously allows one to see a reflection of the white sided elements of both the shoe display and the ceiling that is in sharp contrasts to the red, when seen from the front."

At one end of the shop is a moss covered cash/wrap desk with a green display area for shoes behind it. "This hint of color empha-sizes a sense of nature and makes reference to the outside world further blurring the distinction between inside and outside." For the white seating area/shoe display, elements of Shigeru Ban's 10-Unit-System were produced by Artek and the Yumi black floor stand light fixtures are by FontanaArte.

A bold red wall with white letters spelling out the Camper name greets customers as they enter the store. As they walk through the space the shoe display becomes apparent. Cubbies arranged in a 45 degree angle hold the merchandise.

At the far end of the shop is a moss covered cash/wrap desk with a green display area for shoes behind it. "This hint of color emphasizes a sense of nature and makes reference to the outside world further blurring the distinction between inside and outside."

Shigeru Ban Architects Tokyo, Japan
Dean Maltz Architect New York, NY

DESIGN ARCHITECT
Shigeru Ban Architects

DESIGN PARTNER
Shigeru Ban

MANAGING PARTNER/PRINCIPAL
Dean Maltz

DIRECTOR OF PROJECT
Nina Freedman

ARCHITECT
Ji Young Kim

EXECUTIVE ARCHITECT
Dean Maltz Architect

ENGINEERS
Robert Simon Associates *Structural*
Icor Associates LLC *Mechanical*

CONTRACTOR
Michilli Construction & Consulting

PHOTOGRAPHY
Sanchez y Montero

The Manchester United Experience
The Grand Canal Shoppes, The Venetian, Macao

The entrance is framed with red, concave, hexagonal formwork with the club crest given prominent positioning. Between the generic columns of The Venetian visitors get their first glimpse of the store through geometrically-shaped front windows. The all-important point-of-sale counter, at which tickets for the Experience are also sold, has a curved shape and is sculpted in white Corian. On the wall behind the counter is a red tinted image of the team's stadium in Trafford, England, one of many references to the team's heritage.

The concept driving The Manchester United Experience and Mega store, located in Macao and designed by HEAD Architecture and Design Limited, was to combine a retail setting with an interactive entertainment experience—both celebrating the famed UK football (read soccer in the US) club Manchester United.

Two levels of the Grand Canal Shoppes within The Venetian, a high-end resort, were chosen as the ideal location for the venture. The 6,000 sq. ft. retail component, or Mega store, would be located on the main retail level of the Shoppes, while the larger area needed for the Experience (11,000 sq. ft.), would be located up one level in an area much less expensive in terms of rent. Equally important to the designers was the fact that this real estate arrangement meant that the Experience would be accessed from within—and only from within—the Mega store.

Customer circulation, of paramount importance, was carefully planned and controlled. In addition to the single entrance for both the Mega store and the Experience, the circulation pattern leads customers counter clockwise from the entrance, through the store and on to the sales counter. After purchasing tickets Experience attendees are routed up the staircase located in the middle of the store, through the Experience in a logical manner, and back down to the store via a down-only escalator in the rear of the space. From here visitors must pass through the Mega store, stopping to shop if they wish, before exiting.

The high ceilings of the space allowed the designers to have a circular hole cut in the floor between the Mega store and the Experience and a circular mezzanine level to be created. Here is where attendees of the Experience begin their journey up the stairs and through the mezzanine which serves as a transition area and visual link between store and Experience.

The layout of the store is clean, simple and flexible. Floor units are low to allow customers an uninterrupted view to the back of the store and wall units are likewise capped at a relatively low height (about 8.5 ft.) to provide wall space for easily interchangeable graphics of players and other promotional images. In the front part of the store custom-designed, curved shelving is utilized, while the Nike retail system furniture is used in the remainder of the display areas. Also included in the interior of the store are eye-level advertising, team shots, video displays and life-size images of players with which customers can pose.

Referencing the team's signature "Red Devil" tail is the custom-designed "tail," or sculpture, that hangs from the ceiling and guides customers though the store and back to the sales counter.

On the sales floor underneath the mezzanine The Opus, a gigantic, limited-edition Manchester United Book is on display. Circular seating and videos surround the Opus and entice customers to visit the upper levels. The circular mezzanine level serves as a transition area and visual link between store and Experience—whetting the appetite for what is to come.

HEAD Architecture and Design Limited Hong Kong

DESIGN TEAM
Mike Atkin, Project Director
Max Cheung, Project Team Leader

GRAPHIC DESIGN
Kactus Design Ltd, Hong Kong

INTERACTIVE DESIGNER
MET Studio Design Team

PHOTOGRAPHER
Graham Uden

Reischmann
Kempten, Germany

Working in close collaboration with the Reischmann Group, the Blocher Blocher Partners of Stuttgart have once again created an exciting and enticing home for this sportswear and sporting goods company. Located in Kempten — in the mountain area of Allgäu — this 5,200 sq. meter building (approx. 55,000 sq. ft.) "captivates with its clear geometric forms."

Charcoal-colored frames contrast with the centrally-located, three-story-high display window in front—"modern showcases that guide the view to the presentation of the merchandise and large-scale photos of sports enthusiasts." In contrast, the south part of the structure has smaller scale windows from the third to the fifth floor. Angela Kreutz, a member of the board of the architectural firm adds, "In this way the architecture comes to life and is set into motion, so to speak, a reference to the sporty zeitgeist that Reischmann represents." Shoppers now enter into this soaring space through "friendly entrances flush with the building. In this way, the store invites customers and passers-by to shop." The look and geometry of the exterior façade serves as a framework for the store's interior.

Rough, industrial materials such as concrete and screed are used throughout the different departments and "connect the different sport and fashion offerings with their expressive design."

"The room concept is minimalistic and builds a contrast to individual theme islands on all floors," adds Ms. Kreutz. In some areas the industrial look is complemented with modern materials, while other shops-within-the-shop create a sense of authenticity that connects the store to the town of Kempten and the Allgäu region. One such example is the stylish ski hut that "provides a summit feeling—all inclusive of a cozy fireplace" especially constructed from aged, recycled wood from the area. Another focal element— and a big attraction—is the naturalistic rock "climbing wall" that stretches up to the ceiling of the structure—about 72 feet (22 meters)—and not only affects a mountain ambiance but offers a challenge to the sports-minded and inclined customers. "Thus, a sporty lifestyle is imparted at close range."

With this customer-friendly expansion in Kempten, the 150-year-old family company remains true to its demands for innovation and progress. This sports and trend house combined modern design with authentic atmosphere and was created in five months of construction time.

The architects/designers working with Visplay came up with a unique shop-fitting systems that connects the various departments in the store. It is a grid system made of struts, with which entire walls can be re-functioned to flexible merchandise presentation areas. "In this way products can always be presented at the place where they fit optically and thematically." The system is made of an innovative synthetic-wood compound which is not only resilient but also eco-friendly and underscores Reischmann's desire to be close to nature. Throughout the space the theme of "nature" recurs with presentation fixtures made of recycled old wood and black steel. "These exhibit the same basic design on all floors, but have been embellished individually with natural materials such as bark or stones."

Rough, industrial materials such as concrete and screed are used throughout the different departments and "connect the different sport and fashion offerings with their expressive design."

Blocher Blocher Partners Stuttgart, Germany

ARCHITECTURE & INTERIOR DESIGN
Blocher Blocher Partners, Stuttgart, Germany

SHOPFITTING
Schlegel GmbH & Konrad Knoblauch GmbH

LIGHTING
D&L Lichtplanung

PHOTOGRAPHY
Courtesy of Blocher Blocher

De•Cor
Pasadena, CA

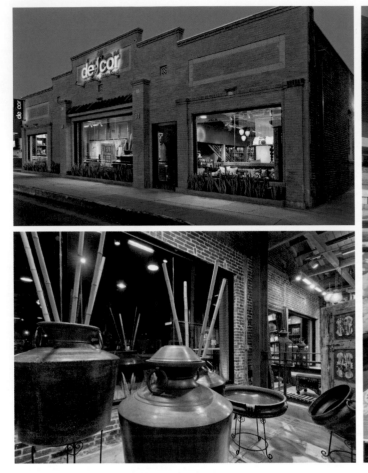

What was formerly a 7,500 sq. ft., early twentieth century antique warehouse has been turned into De•Cor: a magical, mythical world of home fashions and accessories. The large windows set into the brick façade of this free-standing structure offer tantalizing views into the color-filled interior. Inside, the large space is defined by the exposed brick walls, wide swaths of brilliant color, and a restored curved ceiling with sandblasted wood trusses. All the design magic is credited to the Akar Studios of Santa Monica, CA, Sat Garg, the firm's principal and the lead designer Sean Morris.

The designers have provided the following information. "Within this idyllic setting, this retail showroom aspires to create a destination gallery atmosphere for presenting an extensive collection of handcrafted rustic furniture, artifacts and soft furnishings that are primarily sourced from the Indian subcontinent. Although the main space has a few designated areas for permanent use, the walls and the floor space has been designed in such a way as to allow for easy alteration of the layout and groupings of products for sale. For this reason, the retail floor space is reconstructed of stage sets to create flexible combinations and encouraging customer interaction within this eclectic shell."

Because of the variety of product, color and styles, the interior has been kept simple, light and neutral. "A medley of different materials—from polished concrete floors and distressed wood shelves to rustic steel frames, has been used to assist in providing a warm

and inviting atmosphere." One wall, in the center of the space has been painted a bright, strong, fuchsia to "add a visual and sensory interest to capture the eye." The former bathroom that was located behind this wall is now an area where an extensive collection of hand made fabrics is displayed. The shelves in this room, as well as along the perimeter walls of the showroom on which small-sized items and other decorative items are displayed, are of stained plywood and the fixtures are custom made of raw steel.

Some of the large rustic furniture pieces also serve as on-floor displayers and clusters of go-with accessories are assembled into vignette settings to assist shoppers with making selections. Panels of semi-translucent fabrics hang from the wood trussed ceiling to either serve as dividers or backgrounds for the vignettes. Fluorescent lights are combined with spotlights to create a pleasant ambient light as well as pick out special areas of display. Assorted pendant lamps and lanterns also enhance the lighting plan while adding to the ambient look of the space.

Akar Studios has a long and successful background as a designer of award-winning restaurants and cafes, and several have had exotic themes or been highlighted by unique decorative touches. The designers have brought some of that special quality into this retail design and created another award winning space.

Because of the variety of product, color and styles, the interior has been kept simple, light and neutral. "A medley of different materials—from polished concrete floors and distressed wood shelves to rustic steel frames, has been used to assist in providing a warm and inviting atmosphere." One wall in the center of the space has been painted a bright fuchsia to add visual interest.

Akar Studios Santa Monica, CA

DESIGN TEAM
Sat Garg, Principal
Sean W. Morris, Designer

PHOTOGRAPHY
Derek Rath

Loblaws

Maple Leaf Gardens, Toronto, ON Canada

According to Mark Landini, "Our brief was to design and help redefine what an urban supermarket store should look like in today's market. Quite simply, we were to create 'the world's best food store' including active food preparation areas such as a full-scale scratch bakery, 14-chef kitchen, pizzeria, grill, salad and sushi bars, patisserie and confectioner, tea specialist, café, canteen and cooking school, cheese specialist and deli as well as butcher, fishmonger and fresh produce area. We also needed to develop a blueprint that could be implemented in a number of differing sized locations, enhancing and building on Loblaws core brand proposition. Additionally, we were asked to consider how to tell the story of the building's history in an interesting and engaging way."

Maple Leaf Garden, a Canadian iconic landmark in Toronto, has been transformed from an ice hockey "temple" to an 85,000 sq. ft. urban grocery store. The transformation was the work of the Australian design firm Landini Associates under the creative leadership of Mark Landini. What was created here is "an innovative and vibrant urban food shopping experience—an exciting experience for shoppers featuring international design trends such as food theater and the social facility of a town square to elevate the shoppers' experience beyond that of a traditional grocery store."

Working with a small client team, in the 18 month period—from commission to store opening—various concepts were developed and tested in an empty warehouse. "We were keen to create a model that celebrated both the food and the people who make the food whilst at the same time making a visible but 'food friendly' statement that was unmistakably that of Loblaws.

"As for the building's history, we wanted to do this by integrating the stories of the total space as opposed to segregating them in a corner. We chose many different ways of doing this from marking the 'center ice' by aisle 24, exposing the ghosts of walls past, commissioning a sculpture made from old blue stadium chairs, reusing others in the café, reusing stadium lighting in the double-height entrance lobby and reinstating an old mural whilst also celebrating the various cultural and political events both under the canteen tables and on columns within the body of the supermarket."

Graphics and signage were vital components of the overall design. "Much of the directional and departmental signage is outsized to fit within the scale of the building. Many of these were inspired by what you see in a city street. Each area uses a different signage type from the battered tin of the bakery, the timber of the sushi, the impressed concrete of the deli, the bent copper plumbing tube and neon light of the grill to the supergraphics of the perimeter painted over the tile, CFC sheet and plywood substrates."

In summing up what Landini Associates was able to accomplish, Landini said, "I think with Loblaws we have collectively created more than a great food store. We have attempted to make a place that people can use every day in a number of different ways. We re-imagined a market square idea in a densely populated urban context. We also tried to put the 'super' back into supermarket, creating an exciting and interesting place dedicated to the celebration of food. Most supermarkets are designed as 'selling machines' with little thought as to how they can contribute to the soul of the community which they serve. This is something that Loblaws and we were very focused on."

For the visual merchandising and product display, the design team made use of cross merchandising to inspire end usage and suggest menus. "All displays are product led and product intensive and we have avoided display for display sake. We wanted to create excitement at every turn and to that end all the product points are product- and people-focused, from the world's tallest cheese wall and tasting station, the tea wall with over 200 teas, the butcher framed by aged meat cases and the fishmonger with fresh fish tanks."

What makes this layout unique? Landini responded with, "We created a modern version of the market town square. A social hub for the community providing a place to meet, eat and fall in love. A place to sample, watch and be inspired by the food and the food preparation, where people could slow down, browse and learn as well as switching off and socializing. We discarded the plastics, laminates and artificial materials of most supermarkets as well as the generic exposed aggregate concrete floors that litter the continent and chose materials that would age with dignity. We used concrete, stone, ceramic tiles, and multiple timbers as well as a lighting scheme unlike any other found today in these types of environments. The specially designed multiple light sources and fittings were developed for Loblaws to highlight the product and the signage and not to create a bland overall effect. Rather—we wanted the 'light and shade' that one finds in nature —thus providing and encouraging a slower pace than normal."

Landini Associates Sydney, Australia

DESIGN TEAM
Mark Landini, Creative Director
Rikki Landini, Managing Director
Karn Nelson, Strategy & Research
Ian McDougall, Architect
Wayne Cheng, Wenny Arief, Interiors
Mariela Tiqui, Graphics
Emmanuelle Hessel, Studio Manager

BASE BUILDING ARCHITECTS
Buttcon Ltd.

SCULPTURE ARTIST
Steve Richards, Streamliner Fabrication

MURALS
Paul Conway

SIGNAGE
Somerville

PHOTOGRAPHY
Trevor Mein

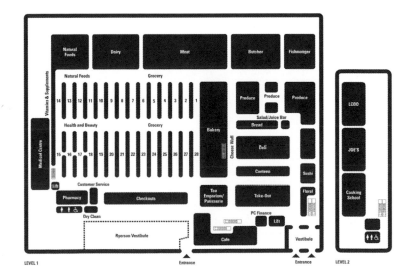

5th Screen Digital Services, Inc.
123 Burlwood Drive, Scotts Valley, CA 95066
PHONE: 408-440-4520/831-818-0584
CONTACT: John Curran, Keith Kelsen
EMAIL: john.curran@5thscreends.com
keith.kelsen@5thscreends.com

You Know Your Business — We Know Digital Engagement
See our ad on page 18

www.5thscreen.com

Certona
9520 Towne Centre Dr., Suite 100, San Diego, CA 92121
P: 858-369-3888 F: 858-369-3880 E: info@certona.com
Direct Contact: **John Glanz** E: **jglanz@certona.com**

Delivering personalized customer experiences for the
world's most popular brands, Certona is the leader for true
omnichannel personalization. Trusted by more than 400 top
ecommerce sites, Certona's real-time personalization
platform increases engagement and conversions by leveraging
real-time behavioral profiling and Big Data to serve up
individualized content, promotional and product
recommendations across all customer touch points.

Learn more: certona.com

EuroShop

The World's Leading Retail Trade Fair
16 – 20 February 2014
Düsseldorf · Germany
www.euroshop.de

**EuroShop 2014/Messe
Dusseldorf North America**
150 N. Michigan Ave., #2920
Chicago, Il 60601
PHONE: 312-781-5180
FAX: 312-781-5188
CONTACT: Eva Rowe
EMAIL: info@mdna.com

EuroShop 2014, The World's
Leading Retail Trade Fair, will be
held from February 16 – 20, 2014 in
Dusseldorf, Germany. EuroShop will
be the international meeting place
for more than 2,000 exhibitors from
50 countries and over 100,000 trade
visitors from around the world.

www.euroshop-tradefair.com

EXPERIENTIAL DESIGN LAB

Experiential Design Lab Private Limited
N-84, Second Floor, Abulfazal
Jamia Nagar, Okhala
New Delhi - 110025, India
PHONE: +91 11 2649 8829
CONTACT: info@experientialdesignlab.com

Experiential Design Lab is an interaction design consultancy focusing on
delivering design-driven stategic innovation to their clients. They deliver
digitally-aided and user-friendly experiences that help businesses establish
integrated customer-brand dialogues. Supported with capabilities to
manufacture tangible interfaces and graphical interfaces, their work has
delivered proven positive impact to their clients.

www.experientialdesignlab.com

UAB "IDW"
Ukmerges str. 248, LT-06120 Vilnius, Lithuania
PHONE: +370 52 470316; FAX: +370 52 478833
EMAIL: office@idw.lt
CONTACT: george@idw-global.us

Big variety of collections or custom-made abstract and realistic
mannequins, torsos and accessories in different finishes
(clear, frost, material covered, vintage or paper Mache looking).
Unbreakable material with Nano-technology based scratch
resistant finish. All production is eco and environment
friendly and 100% recyclable and reusable.

www.idw-global.com

UAB "IDW Metawood"
S.Dariaus ir S.Gireno str. 65A, LT-02189 Vilnius, Lithuania
PHONE: +370 52 306393; FAX: +370 52 164480
EMAIL: info@metawood.idw.lt
CONTACT: ramune@metawood.idw.lt

IDW Metawood specializes in shop fitting solutions from idea to the
trunkey realizations. Our experience extends from single luxury boutique
to global roll outs. We are providing unlimited capacities covered with
highest engineering knowledge and best quality standards. Every
possible material or technology is among our solutions. Each shape
designed could be realized as our flexibility is limitless. Environmental
responsibility is leading us in every single activity. IDW Metawood is
unique sequence of latest fashion creativity, hi end machinery and
sensitive craftsmen touch.

www.idw-global.com

KMDI

PHONE: 913-281-4200; FAX: 913-281-0208
CONTACT: Barry Lakey
EMAIL: barry.lakey@KMDI.net

For nearly 30 years, KMDI has helped America's best known designers and retailers transform environments in just hours. Pre-fabricated, pre-finished MicroLite! soffits, fascias, clouds, trellis, beams, signage, and other decorative architectural elements and displays free designers from the limitations of traditional construction materials, and save retailers time and money.

www.KMDI.net

openeye

London | San Diego | New York

OpenEye

372 Conover St., South Amboy, NJ 08879
PHONE: 877-337-1155
CONTACT: Bryan Meszaros
EMAIL: bmeszaros@openeyeglobal.com.com

OpenEye is a digital media consultancy, which looks to combine consumer insight, technology and creativity to redefine how brands and retailers engage with consumers through a strategic digital in-store experience.

www.openeyeglobal.com

Option III

EMAIL: info@option3display.com
PHONE: 514-823-8820

Our unique finishes and old style craftsmanship marry together as one to create the unimaginable, integrated with the state-of-the-art manufacturing techniques.

www.option3display.com

Primo Vidros Silveira

Av. Dr. Vital Brasil, 647
Butantã – São Paulo – SP 05503-001
PHONE: +55 11-3814-9655
CONTACT: Matheus
EMAIL: matheus@primovidros.com.br

Special Projects and Solutions

www.primovidros.com.br

RCS Innovations

7075 West Parkland Court, Milwaukee, WI 53223
PHONE: 414-354-6900; FAX: 414-354-6930
CONTACT: Larry LaGuardia
EMAIL: larry.laguardia@rcsinnovations.com

RCS is all about Innovations... new ideas, new products and new ways of doing business. Experts in space planning, fixture design and construction, installations and field services: Today you need a partner with a rock solid reputation for quality products and services so you can... "Consider it done."

www.RCSinnovations.com

R+R

Richter+Ratner

Builders Since 1912

Richter+Ratner

45 West 36th Street, 12th Foor
New York, NY 10018
PHONE: 212-936-4500; FAX: 212-710-5858
EMAIL: info@richterratner.com

www.richterratner.com

Studio Serradura

88, St. Artur de Almeida – Vila Mariana, Sao Paulo, Brazil
PHONE: +55-11-3881-3990
EMAIL: comunicacao@studioserradura.com
CONTACT: Rafael Serradura
EMAIL: rafael@studioserradura.com

Being extraordinary is the simple fact of not being another one! Create, re-create, develop, inspire, breath, live, build, run away from the obvious...have fun.

www.studioserradura.com
studioserradura.tumblr.com

Stylmark, Inc.
PO Box 32006, 6536 Main Street NE
Minneapolis, MN 55432
PHONE: 800-328-2495; FAX: 763-574-1415
CONTACT: Carrie Harvey Schnabel
EMAIL: info@stylmark.com

Stylmark is a versatile manufacturer that creates the spectrum of essential elements — to create comprehensive and distinctive lifestyle environments. Whether your expertise lies in design, planning, manufacturing or installation, you can rely on Stylmark to collaborate with you in designing, integrating, and delivering the best possible solution to ensure your business needs and objectives are met.

www.stylmark.com

Toshiba Global Commerce Solutions
3039 Cornwallis Road, Bldg. 307
Research Triangle Park, NC 27709
PHONE: 800-426-4968
CONTACT: http://www2.toshibagcs.com/l/17552/2012-10-31/9g2

Toshiba Global Commerce Solutions is retail's first choice for integrated in-store solutions. With a global team of dedicated business partners, we deliver innovative commerce solutions that transform checkout, provide seamless consumer interactions and optimize retail operations that are changing the retail landscape. To learn more, visit www.toshibagcs.com.

www.toshibagcs.com

Atmospheric Experience Design Group

PHONE: 858-208-0838
EMAIL: info@designagi.com
CONTACT: Brian Dyches
www.designagi.com

Atmospheric provides a broad range of retail & design consultancy services to help retailers/brands and shopping center developers remain competitive and achieve their experience goals. *Our range of services we provide.*

- Customer Experience Analysis
- Brand and Retail Concepts
- Intelligence
- Digital Strategy & Design
- Retail Consulting
- Training & Seminars

For more details please contact Brian Dyches.

RDI Media / RSD Publishing

302 Fifth Avenue, New York, NY 10001
PHONE: 212-279-7000; FAX: 212-279-7014
CONTACT: John Burr
EMAIL: jburr@rdimedia.com

For more than 75 years it has been our mission to inspire and educate retail professionals and designers, keeping them up-to-date with what's new and ground-breaking in interior design and architecture. Our bimonthly publication, *Retail Design International,* is the premier periodical for seeing the best in retail design, visual merchandising and display. Visit our site to learn about the many benefits of subscribing to *Retail Design International,* see our many books, and learn about opportunities to have your own work published.

www.rdimedia.com

Retail Design Institute™

The Retail Design Institute represents the retail industry's creative professionals and was founded in 1961 to be a collaborative community where ideas, knowledge and passion would be shared at a local level and enable our members to fulfill the fast-paced planning and design needs of retail. The Institute reaches out to the retail community through chapter meetings; providing workshops and seminars, highlighting new and noteworthy trends, and recognizing accomplishments in retailing and store design.

Our mission is to promote the advancement and collaborative practice of creating selling environments.

Today, our membership includes architects, graphic designers, lighting designers, interior designs, store planners, visual merchandisers, resource designers, brand strategists, educators, trade partners, editors and publishers, and students. The Institute supports the career of our membership; providing continuing education to improve the skill sets of working professionals, enhancing and certifying design credentials, and informing the industry that our members are serious about the design of high quality, cost effective and financially viable retail environments. Being part of our global organization provides the opportunity to connect with design professionals around the world, and share in the market intelligence of new projects and emerging design trends in other countries.

Visit www.retaildesigninstitute.org to learn more and join.

Andrew McQuilkin, FRDI
International President
Retail Design Institute

INDEX OF DESIGN FIRMS